Garden of Hope

**Essays
From an Award-Winning
Alzheimer's Blog**

By

L. S. Fisher

MoZark

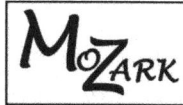

www.MozarkPress.com

Published by Mozark Press, www.Mozarkpress.com
PO Box 1746, Sedalia, MO 65302

Cover Photo: L.S. Fisher taken at Sedalia Walk to End Alzheimer's

Acknowledgement: Cover design and book layout by H.D. Ream

DISCLAIMER: *Statements or opinions expressed in the stories and articles of this publication are those of the author and do not necessarily represent the views or positions of any person or entity associated with publication of the book or the Alzheimer's Association.*

ISBN: 978-0-9844385-9-4

Dedication

The Early Onset Alzheimer's Blog is dedicated to Jimmy D. Fisher and to all whose lives have been disrupted by a debilitating disease and to their families.

Other Titles by L. S. Fisher

Alzheimer's Anthology of
Unconditional Love

Early Onset Blog
Essays from an Online Journal
(Ozark Writers League 2010 Book of the Year)

Early Onset Blog
The Friendship Connection and Other Essays

Early Onset Alzheimer's
Encourage, Inspire, and Inform

Early Onset Alzheimer's
My Recollections, Our Memories

Focus on the Positive

Available at www.lsfisher.com

Table of Contents

Introduction

More than five million Americans have Alzheimer's disease. As we baby boomers age, the numbers are going to escalate unless a cure and effective treatment can be developed. Without advocates to forward the cause, and dire need, of research, millions more will fall to this incurable disease.

A cure for Alzheimer's has long been a daunting task for researchers, but it is by no means a hopeless task. Great strides have been made through research, and a common dietary supplement seems to be the first ever treatment that slows the progression of the disease. This is a huge development!

I love sharing this kind of news through my early onset Alzheimer's blog. In 2008, I took on the task of writing a realistic blog about Alzheimer's and caregiving to not only inform, but also to inspire and encourage. I began my blog after the death of my husband Jim as I embarked on the new unchartered waters of widowhood. No longer a caregiver, I threw more of my energy into Alzheimer's advocacy.

It was important to me to stay connected with the caregivers I had come to know and love. In addition to caregivers, I became acquainted with people living with Alzheimer's disease who inspired me much more than I could ever inspire them.

A blog accomplishes nothing if no one reads it. Fortunately, over the years, more and more people discover the blog. The comments I hear from new readers are "an unusual approach," or, more recently, "unique information."

Just like flowers in a garden, the essays I write are varied. Some are pretty like roses, while others are more functional, like marigolds. As a whole they make up a Garden of Hope. Even knowing Alzheimer's, we find reasons to laugh, friends to rely on, and hope that although the garden may become bedraggled, spring will bring renewal.

~ Linda Fisher

It's a New Year, A New Day
A New Year's Day

How do you feel about New Year's Day? Are you excited and hopeful or have you become jaded about the entire resolution thing?

I watched part of the celebration in New York City and, of course, wanted to see the ball drop. Is it just me, or have they really blocked the view now with all the signs and advertisement? Last year, for some reason, I decided they had not shown the ball drop because I couldn't see it. Paying closer attention this time, I saw the ball disappear behind the countdown clock and a tower's worth of advertisements. Does anyone else think this is a rip off?

In addition, the host and hostess yammered on about how bad 2011 was and how hopeful everyone had been last year that the New Year would be better, but 2012 disappointed everyone too. And why did we think that 2013 would be any different? Geeze, why don't we start out with a negative attitude—I'm sure that will make it all better.

Perhaps to some people, New Year's Day becomes a lot like birthdays—the more you have of them, the less special they become. Well, sometimes if you have enough birthdays you get to have a big birthday celebration for landmark years—80, 85, 90, 95, etc. The New Year, on the other hand, is always the first chapter of another book.

I don't know about you, but I always find New Year's Day a time to plan ways to make it a better year. I cannot help it if I'm an optimist, and really why would I want to change that? I know it's hard to feel optimistic, especially if you or a loved one are bogged down with depression or dealing with a serious illness.

Jim had health problems for many years and suffered from depression. Life sometimes seemed overwhelming for him. The one thing that kept him going was what he deemed "something to look forward to." For him, something to look forward to was usually a road trip to visit his beloved family in Oregon or to camp in the Colorado Rockies. Weeks ahead of the trip, Jim would begin to spit shine and pack the van with everything we could possibly need.

One of the saddest things about Jim's dementia was that he didn't seem to be able to look forward to traveling anymore. We went to Colorado for a few years after Jim showed signs of dementia. After a total fiasco trying to pitch our tent, we stayed in hotels when we went to Estes Park. It wasn't quite the same, and eventually, we substituted Branson vacations for longer trips.

Jim is the reason I love to travel. I'll admit that our early trips were pretty much an endurance test. With limited funds and not so dependable vehicles, some of our trips were the kind of experiences that seem better in retrospect than at the time. Later, we learned to slow down and enjoy the scenery, or stop to see the local sights along the way.

Am I excited about 2013? You bet! This is going to be a year for a major life event for me. I plan to retire from my day job after thirty-three years, which will give me more time to spend with family, to travel, and to write. I've been so busy trying to fit everything in that the only time I've relaxed in months was while I was trying to fight off a bad cold. I sat on the couch and watched hours and hours of shows on my DVR. I watched an entire season of *Leverage* in two days!

The truth is that I have so little time to watch TV that I record everything and usually watch it when I should be in bed sleeping.

So, as Jim would say, I really have something to look forward to this year—time, the most precious of God's gift. It is up to me to take it when it is offered.

Find a Friend Friday

I am blessed to have a lot of friends, and hope that you do too. If you are like me, you hesitate to ask friends for a favor and would much rather be the one paying it forward.

Those of you who know me, and who follow my blog have already figured out that although I'm involved in many things, Alzheimer's and dementia are my passions.

I've been blogging since 2008, but my mission started when my husband, Jim, was diagnosed with an Alzheimer's type of dementia at age forty-nine. Now, people who, like me, have had their heart broken by a disease that slowly steals a loved one away daily visit the little blog I began. The circle of family and friends and their support is so important. They are the ones that keep you going and laughing. Their hugs are much like the mother's kiss that really can make it better.

Early Onset Alzheimer's blog has been nominated by Healthline for the best health blog of 2012 contest with a $1,000 prize. Currently, I'm in the top ten out of 300+ blogs. The competition is fierce and my friends and family have kept me there for over a week. Thank you, if you have been casting your vote each day.

If each of you will find a friend today to vote for Early Onset Alzheimer's blog, I think I can maintain my third place position and even move forward. Who knows, if we double the votes with one friend each, we could even win this contest!

Thank you for your support, and I hope the friend you find today is a blessing in your life.

The Alzheimer's Advocacy Forum
Celebrates Silver

Linda Fisher & Robert Fischer
Advocacy Forum 2012

When the Alzheimer's Association began operations in 1980, they made it very clear that Alzheimer's wasn't just a joke for late night TV. What people previously thought of as senility had a name. Forgetfulness might not be mental lapses, it could be a disease that destroyed brain cells.

The mission of the Alzheimer's Association is "A world without Alzheimer's." They have a twofold goal of finding a cure through research and providing support and services to the families dealing with dementia.

The Alzheimer's Association is now the largest non-profit funder of Alzheimer's research. They offer grants to scientists for promising studies. Along with the important funding of research, the families are not forgotten. The Association provides strategies to help caregivers cope with daily challenges and a 24/7 helpline for those overwhelming moments. They have given a voice and a face to the more than five million Americans with Alzheimer's.

My personal involvement with the Alzheimer's Association began before Jim had received a diagnosis. The first call to the Mid-Missouri Chapter assured me that this organization would help us. They threw out the life-line and we grabbed on and never let go.

Fast forward to April 2001—Penny Braun, executive director, of the Mid-Missouri Chapter invited me to attend the annual Alzheimer's Public Policy Forum with her. I immediately accepted. I had been a faithful Memory Day participant at the state level, and I was eager to take advocacy to the national level.

When we arrived in D.C., cherry blossoms were in full bloom. The Forum was a whirlwind of activity and my head was spinning from the staggering statistics. There is something about visiting senators and representatives that make you want to know the hard facts to convince them that Alzheimer's research is woefully underfunded. It doesn't take long to discover that one of the most important jobs of an advocate is to tell your personal story. You provide the answer to: Why are you here, and why do you care so much?

This year, the Alzheimer's Advocacy Forum will celebrate its silver anniversary! Yesterday I received a personal email from Monica Moreno, director of early stage initiatives for the Alzheimer's Association at their national office in Chicago. "Congratulations on your nomination!" in response to Early Onset Alzheimer's blog's nomination for Best Health Blog of 2012 contest. If I win the contest and the $1,000 prize, I plan to help fund my annual trip to the Advocacy Forum.

Moreno continued to share some exciting news about the forum. "I was also thrilled to see that for the past thirteen years, you have been an active participant at the Alzheimer's Association Advocacy Forum which is again being held in Washington, D.C., this coming April. I think you'll be happy to know that in honor and recognition of our 25th anniversary of the

Advocacy Forum, the Association is waiving the registration fee for every attendee!"

Free registration! Love it. I believe in the Forum enough that I have paid my own way for most of the years I've attended. Together, we can accomplish our goals. We've fought to keep funding for Alzheimer's research through years of budget slashing. I am pleased that I was one of the Alzheimer's advocates with boots on the ground advocating for the "National Alzheimer's Project" and the "National Alzheimer's Plan." It is heartening to know that we personally asked for and received support for this important legislation.

One of the important aspects of advocacy is to work with legislators without regard to political party. I enjoy meeting with my senator, Claire McCaskill, and my representative, Vicky Hartzler. I've developed good relationships with the health aides too over the years. Most legislators like to meet personally with constituents, but sometimes it is impossible. Aides play an important role in getting legislation passed and are typically well informed.

Alzheimer's can be a lonely disease, but one of the benefits of the forum is building close relationships with other advocates. At the very first forum, I met Jane, Kathy, Sarah, and Ralph. I bonded with these four caregivers in a special way. Each year, I've met special people that enrich my life.

We've accomplished much over the past twenty-five years, but there is still work to be done! I'll be in Washington, D.C., April 22-24 for the silver anniversary celebration. We join together to continue the fight on Capitol Hill for legislation and funding for Americans with Alzheimer's and for their families.

Save the Day Sunday

Do you remember Mighty Mouse and his proclamation that "Here I come to save the day!" He was just a mouse, but he was mighty. A pint-sized superhero. Guess that just goes to prove that you don't have to be big, or well known, to make a difference. Each one of us can "save the day" for someone. We can say a kind word or do a good deed. It doesn't always take something big to make a difference, it can be just a small thing like a hug, a smile, a note, or a quick phone call to say "I'm thinking of you" or "I love you."

Here's to hoping you can be a superhero, if even in a pint-sized, or half-pint-sized way. Crank up that smile and be prepared to pass around the hugs as needed.

Movin' On Up Monday
Alzheimer's Advocacy

Do you remember the TV show *The Jeffersons*? It had some great characters with George, "Weesie," and the maid Florence. The whole idea of the show was that they were moving up in the world. Their dreams had come true.

Monday always gets a bad rap. Instead of seeing it as a time to jump in and get things done, we view it as a day that takes more coffee and more willpower than any other day of the week.

Today, the first Monday of 2013, instead of dreading the day, let's think of it as the perfect opportunity to use our talents and skills to advance to a new level—to step up and move on up.

Tenacious Tuesday

Tenacity is a characteristic that has a positive impact on a caregiver's effectiveness. Alzheimer's disease can last for decades, and a tenacious caregiver has the staying power to persevere without faltering.

One of the most tenacious people I have known in my life was my mother-in-law. She tackled life with a bulldogged determination. When Jim developed dementia, she was a rock every step of the journey. From the early stages to the nursing home years, her unconditional loving care never once wavered.

Today, I salute my mother-in-law and all the other tenacious caregivers who have loved ones with Alzheimer's and other terminal diseases. It takes a special kind of person to overcome adversity and still live life to the fullest.

Welcome Mat Wednesday

Today, I'm rolling out the welcome mat for my new blog followers—networked, regular followers, Pinterest, email, bookmarking the blog, or through one of the rebroadcasted postings. I appreciate everyone who reads Early Onset Alzheimer's blog and hope you find the blog inspirational and informative.

The blog is written in a "user friendly" style even when I discuss health news. I don't use medical jargon. I am not a medical professional and don't like needles. The sight of blood makes me sick to my stomach. I do have an insatiable curiosity about any breakthroughs in Alzheimer's research and therapies. I also have first-hand knowledge of being a primary caregiver for a loved one with dementia and understand the turmoil a caregiver endures.

Most of the new traffic to my blog and Facebook is because of the Healthline Best Health Blog of the Year Contest, but I hope that after the contest is over, everyone continues to visit.

And on this middle day of the workweek, I throw the virtual door open to welcome to all who enter the blogosphere to read Early Onset Alzheimer's blog.

Take Control Thursday

When your loved one has dementia, you may feel life is getting out of control. You spend all your time putting out fires, and never have time to relax and enjoy your hobbies.

I gave some thought to some of the ways I dealt with Jim's dementia and shortened the list to five items that I found most helpful.

1. Prioritize. Important things at the top of the list. Of course, you will need to allocate time to spend with your loved one with dementia, but you need to schedule breaks too. Put aside time to spend with your family and friends. You can become so wrapped up in being a caregiver that you neglect the other people you love.

2. Adjust Your Attitude: You are not able to control the disease, or your loved one, but you can take control of how you react. I think some of the best advice I ever received about how to deal with behaviors was "So what?" When something happens, and no one is in danger, ask yourself "so what?" you might be surprised at how many times it isn't really important at all.

3. Spend time with hobbies or pastimes you love. If you can't find a relative to stay with your loved one, check into hiring a caregiver. If you don't have respite from caregiving, you will become so stressed that you won't be the excellent caregiver you want to be.

4. Allow downtime every day. Take a walk, go to the gym, read—schedule at least an hour a day to indulge in relaxation.

5. Write. Make lists: to-do lists, wish lists, lists of your loved one's medications and symptoms to help you during your doctor visits. As important as making lists is to keep a journal where you can write about your emotions. Writing is therapeutic and helps mend the rifts in your soul.

Be thankful for the time God has given you and regain control of your destiny, one day at a time. Have a great Thursday! May today be the beginning of a new era for you.

Foggy Friday

There's something about this time of year, when a little rain mixed with unseasonably warm weather produces fog. I'll admit I'm not a big fan of fog. For one thing, it's a little spooky to be driving along and hit a heavy patch of fog. For some reason this always seems a little bit like driving into the *Twilight Zone*. Makes me halfway expect to hear strange music and to see Rod Serling, dressed in a suit and tie, standing alongside the road ready to hint at what's really going on in the depths of the thickest fog.

Fog scares me—especially since the night I was driving along a gravel road after a visit with Jim at the nursing home and hit fog so thick I couldn't see anything. I stopped and with trembling fingers dialed my son's phone. I was afraid someone would come along and ram into me.

"If you can't see anything then surely no one else is driving either," he said.

While I sat there waiting for the fog to lift, I couldn't help but think about how Alzheimer's is like a fog blanketing cognitive skills. Sometimes, fog just drifts in and out, but other times, it halts us in our tracks.

After a few long moments, the world became visible, and I could see the road. I drove to my son's house. When I worked up the nerve to head on home, he still thought it was risky for me to drive, so he led the way. His taillights were like beams shining from a lighthouse directing me to safety.

You can be that beacon for your loved one when the fog is the thickest.

Paying it Forward

During the holidays, you hear many heartwarming stories about people paying it forward. McDonald's and Starbucks have both reported people in the drive-thru paying for the next car, and that person continues paying it forward. Chain reactions of generosity have been known to last for hours. It is really cool to hear about these fast food pay-it-forward lines, and it helps restore faith in human kindness and thoughtfulness, but real pay-it-forward heroes are those who make it a way of life.

Volunteering is the best way of paying it forward and is one of the reasons that people volunteer. There may be a few glory-grabbing volunteers, mostly high profile people, who show up for an event or catastrophe for a photo op. But those are the exceptions. Most volunteers fly far below the radar, doing their best to give more to the world than they take.

Some people admire volunteers for doing what they don't feel like they have the time to do. The thing I have noticed is that the busiest people make the best volunteers.

What makes a person volunteer? It could be an internal desire to help others, but often a major event spurs us to take action.

I am a prime example. At one time, I never volunteered for anything. I figured my life was busy enough with a full time job and family to take care of. I was fully aware I didn't have time to volunteer for anything, and when pulled into helping, I wasn't always the most cheerful or willing person in the group. Sure, I wanted to do a good job, but often my heart just wasn't in it.

My entire attitude and outlook changed when Jim developed dementia. The more I learned about the disease, the more motivated I was to do whatever I could to help. My first true heartfelt volunteer work was our local Memory Walk. I jumped in with both feet and spent countless hours strategizing how to have a successful walk.

Since then, volunteering has become a way of life for me. I only volunteer for causes and organizations I believe in—and only for tasks I think I can complete, and complete competently. If it falls out of my area of expertise, then I decline because I don't want to bungle the job.

Acts of kindness for another, without thought of how it can benefit you, is paying it forward. All you have to do is look around for opportunities. Do you have an elderly neighbor who needs someone to help with yard work? Do you know a caregiver that needs to run to the store, but must have someone to watch a loved one with dementia for a short time? Maybe you know the server at your favorite restaurant has financial problems, yet she serves you with a smile. What if you left her a $50 tip instead of $5?

Recently, I saw a post on Facebook, that said, "Taking this challenge from a friend: 2013 Creative Pay-It-Forward. The first five people to comment on this status will receive from me, sometime in the next calendar year, a gift—perhaps a book or baked goods, or a candle, music,— a surprise! There will likely be no warning & it will happen whenever the mood strikes me. The catch? Those five people must make the same offer as their status."

My immediate reaction: "I'm in!" I reposted and now I have five friends that will probably forget all about this. They are going to be pleasantly surprised to receive an unexpected gift, and I will have the pleasure of deciding what and when.

Paying it forward isn't about big things at all, it is about little kindnesses to brighten someone's day. It isn't about getting a pat on the back, it's about just doing what feels right in your heart. Paying it forward will help the giver as much as it helps the person who receives.

Just a Test

I grew up during the cold war era, and it wasn't unusual to be watching TV and see a test pattern pop up on the screen and hear a shrill tone scream an alarm. When I was a kid, my heart would thud in my chest if I heard the tone without the preamble, "This is a test of the Emergency Broadcast System." I always felt relieved when at the end the words, "This is only a test" were repeated.

Eventually, the rules changed, and the EBS was used to warn of impending natural disasters, and in our area, that would be tornadoes. I didn't get the memo about the new use for the notification system. The first time I heard, "We interrupt this broadcast," followed with a tone that could make a dog howl, I spent thirty long seconds imagining we were going to be a nation of crispy critters as soon as the nuclear mushroom cloud radiated us. I was one darned happy kid to find out it was merely a tornado in a different county.

Of course, tests later caused a different kind of anxiety. I always over-studied the material to make a good grade on tests. I hated to miss any questions and a *B* just wasn't an acceptable grade. The problem I found with knowing the material so well is that sometimes I would miss a question because of a nuance that made the answer technically incorrect. It seems that other kids just skimmed the surface and marked it, but I would know that part of the answer was wrong.

Not long ago, my daughter-in-law and I were discussing the answers to a quiz, and I discovered that she was a lot like me when it came to analyzing multiple-choice answers. We tried to figure out why a teacher would give two answers that could technically be right, but expect the student to decipher which answer she expected. One question had to do with what you would say to a new mother who had cut down on cigarettes. One answer was to tell her "It is good you cut down, but you are probably still getting nicotine." Because of the word "probably," we knew that had to be the wrong answer. Wrong! That was the teacher's choice.

Now, most of the tests I have are medical tests and you can't study for those. It seems that the older I get, the more determined physicians are that they can surely to goodness find something wrong with me. By the time they poke and prod, take a few vials of blood, and run tubes with a little camera down my throat or up my ahem, I don't stand a chance. Sure enough, they always find something. What happened to the days when I felt pretty darned good and was blissfully unaware that things were falling apart on the inside?

When Jim started having memory problems, our family doctor sent him to a psychologist, who in turn sent Jim for a battery of tests. The results of those tests proved to be a turning point in our lives. I knew Jim was having problems, but the tests showed he had dementia. He couldn't do simple math, count backwards from ten, or name any words that began with the letter "a." Jim had done a good job of covering his deficits, and I was shocked to learn about the problems he had with abstract thinking.

Jim became part of a study for a Phase III drug. He was tested during each follow up visit with the neurologist. They let me stay with him during the testing.

"What season is it?" the nurse asked.

"I have no idea," Jim replied.

"Did you wear a coat today?" she asked as a cue.

"Yes."

"What season do you think it is if you are wearing a coat?"

"I have no idea."

"Do you know where you are?"

"A hospital."

"Do you know what city this is?"

"Yes." He couldn't come up with a name, but was confident he knew where he was.

"Do you know where the stamp goes on this envelope?" She handed him an envelope.

"Right there," he said pointing to the upper right hand corner. He gave me a look, like he thought she might be just a bit stupid to not know where the stamp went.

It was a test, right? Just a test. So why did it bring tears to my eyes?

Sometimes You Just Have a Bad Day

When I first met Jim, he was twenty-two years old, played a guitar, and sang country songs. He heavily favored Buck Owens, Merle Haggard, George Jones, and other old time country greats. Jim had a knack for hearing a song once and being able to sing it perfectly. It never ceased to amaze me that he could learn lyrics so effortlessly.

In the eighties, we began to take annual vacations to the Rockies. One day we walked into a shop in Estes Park where they were playing a version of "Happy Trails" that obviously was not Roy Rodgers and Dale Evans.

"Who is singing that song?" Jim asked the owner of the shop.

"That's Michael Martin Murphey," she said.

It was love at first sound for Jim, and Michael Martin Murphey became his favorite singer. His repertoire now included "Ghost Riders in the Sky," "Tumbling Tumbleweeds," and other cowboy songs. One day, he started singing an obscure song, "I Ain't Had a Good Day" about a cowboy whose day was so bad he was ready to shoot anyone who got in his way and then kick dirt on them. After dementia robbed Jim of the lyrics to many songs, he could remember that one.

Yesterday, I thought about the bad day song. I had a frustrating day at work and on my lunch hour, I checked on the Healthline contest and was dismayed to see that my blog had dropped from second to third. Although my voters rallied, we kept losing ground. Since Early Onset Alzheimer's blog had been in second for quite some time, I kept noticing my voters voting for the second place blog…which was a different one than they intended.

The day wore on, just getting worse on all fronts. I was about to the meltdown point when the workday ended. I was the last one out the door and saw the day's mail still on the shelf. I thought I had time to take it to the post office and still make it to my granddaughter's basketball game.

Okay, had I not taken the mail, I wouldn't have been on Broadway at all. I left the post office, fastened my seatbelt, drove the correct direction on the one-way street, stopped at all stop signs, signaled my turns even when no one was around, stopped at the light and made a right turn onto Broadway driving the speed limit. Obeying each and every law as far as I could tell. So why did the city police officer turn on his lights? Yep. He must mean me, so I found a side street and pulled over.

"Ma'am, you were driving on the white line," he said. I must have had a blank look on my face because he added, "The one on the right side of the street."

Okay. As I dug out my driver's license and insurance card, I told him, "I've not been having a good day." And now, it just went from bad to worse. Getting stopped for driving on my side of the road, what's up with that? Was he afraid I was going to mess up the paint job? If they had those little rumble strips, I'd have known I was touching the white line.

"I'm going to accept this insurance card although it's expired." This whole insurance card thing annoys me. They can check everything else with your driver's license, why can't they put insurance info on their computers? I've had insurance with the same company, without a single lapse, for the past forty years. So why do I have to keep changing those cards?

After the delay, no ticket, I made it to the ballgame on time. All parking lots were jam-packed. I found a back parking lot, which not only was full, a truck was blocking the road out of the lot. Now, *he* deserved a ticket! I was able to drive off the pavement to get out of the lot. My first break of the day happened then as someone backed out of a parking place.

Once I was inside the gym, I found my son and daughter-in-law. I couldn't help but repeat the words Jim so often sang and greeted them with, "I'm telling you friends, I ain't had a good day." And, I sincerely meant it.

Being a Caregiver Isn't What You Do
It Is Who You Are

Being a caregiver to a loved one who has dementia isn't a job that anyone wants, and yet 15 million Americans fill those unpaid positions. This army of caregivers is made up of various friends and relatives who battle the around-the-clock attention that a person with dementia requires.

The Alzheimer's journey is a long and complex route. It begins with small lapses and glitches that can be overlooked or explained away. It is easy to be in denial that something major is going on, and you just tend to muddle through each day as it comes.

By the time, the symptoms become more obvious, you go through an entire battery of tests to rule out any diseases that can be treated. As in any diagnostic process, you will go through highs and lows. Some physicians will analyze the tests results and give you different answers. One might say, "It's low blood sugar and as soon as you treat that, the symptoms will go away." Another might say, "Get your affairs in order while you still can." Throughout the early diagnostic process, the caregiver shares the anxiety, the fear, and the loss with a loved one. Later in the disease, the caregiver bears those anxieties alone.

When your loved one has Alzheimer's or other related dementia, caregiving becomes an all-consuming responsibility. If your parent has Alzheimer's, you find that your roles have reversed and you feel like the parent. If it is your spouse, you miss the special bond you had and find your love changing from a reciprocal relationship to one where you expect nothing in return.

Most people look at a caregiver and think he or she is a person who feeds, bathes, toilets, and watches over the person with dementia. They see the physical side of caregiving as the overwhelming responsibility. They see a caregiver who looks exhausted from the physical demands and lack of sleep. They may even understand the mental strain of trying to keep a loved one safe: taking car keys away from someone who has driven for many years or installing special locks or alarms to keep them from wandering away and getting lost.

What the outsider cannot see is the pain and stress that threatens to overwhelm the caregiver's soul. They cannot see the inch-by-inch losses that make each day a new challenge. They cannot see the inner strength that keeps the caregiver going against all odds. By this point, the caregiver knows there is no cure, no effective treatment, and no hope of survival for her loved one.

The outsider may wonder, *why bother? It's a losing battle.* These are the same people who won't go to visit because, "He doesn't know who I am and won't remember if I've been there." Hogwash! People with dementia might not be able to say your name or even recognize you, but they know when someone cares enough to spend time with them, bring them a milkshake, give them a hug, or make them laugh. No, they don't need anyone visiting who is going to resent spending time with them or upsets them, but someone who cares enough to learn how to communicate with a person who has dementia is always a welcome visitor.

After Jim's disease progressed and I couldn't provide the kind of care he needed at home, people used to ask if Jim knew who I was. Jim was silent the last few years of his life, so I wasn't sure whether he remembered my name or that I was his wife. It actually became irrelevant. What he did know was that I came to see him every day and that I loved him. It wasn't important that he remembered me, but that I, and the rest of our family, never forgot him.

Studies show that the hardest part of being a caregiver is grief. A caregiver's grief is insidious, sneaking up and attacking unexpectedly. For a caregiver to remain healthy, he or she needs to find solace in the fact that the person with dementia is taken care of physically and showered with love.

Caregiving with love isn't what you do; it is who you are. You owe it to yourself, and to your loved one, to keep the faith that live *is* good, but some of us have bumpier roads for our journey.

Inquiring Minds Want to Know
Is It Really Alzheimer's?

L.S. Fisher
Alzheimer's Advocate

There are two kinds of people when it comes to health issues—those who want to know everything and those who want to know nothing. One group falls into the category of die-hard realists and the other is filled with those in denial.

There aren't any simple answers when it comes to health. A visit to a physician can make or break your day, and sometimes your spirit, depending on how he presents your health issues. But even more important is how *you* interpret the diagnosis you are given.

Getting an Alzheimer's diagnosis is a long and arduous process. An entire battery of tests, scans, and evaluations are used to determine if you might have a treatable condition. Once other conditions—thyroid, drug interaction, vitamin deficiencies, too much calcium—are ruled out, your physician may give you a diagnosis of Alzheimer's.

Hundreds of other related dementias exist besides Alzheimer's. Since Alzheimer's is the most common cause of dementia, it is the usual diagnosis. As the disease progresses, the type of dementia may become more evident as frontotemporal dementia, Lewy body disease, vascular or other common dementias. Some conditions can be determined by genetic testing— familial early onset Alzheimer's or Huntington's, for example.

For millions, the exact cause of dementia remains unknown or is determined by autopsy. We chose autopsy to get an exact cause of Jim's dementia, which turned out to be corticobasal degeneration. Since Jim was diagnosed with Alzheimer's, and not too many people know what corticobasal degeneration is, it is easier to say he had an Alzheimer's type of dementia.

A drug that allows a PET scan to detect Alzheimer's plaques is under debate. The controversy is whether Medicare should pay for the $3,000 test. Opponents to the test say that it won't help. I was floored to see the quote in the national article was from a physician in my hometown. The quote: "There's never been a study that asked whether patients do better as a result of florbetapir testing," said David Kuhlmann, a neurologist at Bothwell Regional Health Center in Sedalia, Missouri.

Okay, we all know there is no cure for Alzheimer's and treatment is for symptoms only. Because of the bleak prognosis, no one seems to see a need for an accurate diagnosis. But early diagnosis is crucial in irreversible dementia for several reasons. First, it is important for a person with dementia to make important life decisions while they still can. Jim and I both signed advance directives, durable power of attorneys, and wills. Had we owned more, estate planning would have been even more important. Second, treatments are more effective in the early stages of the disease.

Putting aside all reasons for a diagnosis, and how it could actually help, there is the matter of cost, and Medicare needs to avoid unnecessary expense. So, this test costs $3,000. Expensive enough, I'd say. I'm going to throw out a ballpark figure of $20,000 to complete all the testing to attempt to rule out Alzheimer's. In our case, most of that was paid through private insurance, and out of pocket, rather than Medicare.

Once we ruled out other conditions that could cause reversible dementia, we purchased expensive drugs that had no effect whatsoever on Jim, other than side-effects, because he didn't have amyloid plaques. Of course, we didn't know that until after he died. A $3,000 PET scan to find out his dementia was not Alzheimer's, as diagnosed, could have saved many more thousands on drugs and costly emergency room visits.

I can think of a lot of scary diagnoses and can narrow down the ones that would make me take stock and reevaluate my entire life and lifestyle. Alzheimer's type of dementia, cancer, and heart disease would be at the top of the list. I would only hope that if I were ever diagnosed with any of those three, I would be a realist and want to know every treatment available and evaluate my options to have the best life possible.

I'll admit that Alzheimer's, or any related dementia, scares me the most. I've seen it, felt it, and breathed it throughout Jim's journey. Through my volunteer and advocacy work, I've met many people with Alzheimer's and their caregivers who face the diagnosis with grace and unbelievable courage. Alzheimer's affects not only your body, but your skills, communication, and a lifetime of memories that connect you to your loved ones. Have you ever thought about how empty you would feel without memories?

Isn't it important to know what is wrong with our health, so we can either make it right, or at least do what we can?

Fighting the Paper War

For the past two days, I've been fighting the paper war, and though I've won a couple of minor skirmishes, I cannot say that I'm anywhere close to winning. It seems that I have bags, boxes, storage tubs, file cabinets, and various temporary containers chocked full of paperwork.

I'll be the first to admit that I get totally aggravated with myself when I can't find an important piece of paper. When I'm being good, I file things away, or at least put common papers in their designated spot. On most days, I throw my mail on the end table and may or may not look at it, much less sort it.

Considering how hectic my life is, it makes perfect sense that I work in organized chaos most of the time. I put one project aside to work on another with a shorter deadline. I shuffle bags containing my writing group, Alzheimer's board, Walk to End Alzheimer's, Sedalia Business Women, Business Women of Missouri, and writing projects. Sometimes, I feel like throwing everything in the air and working on it randomly.

Yesterday, I tackled some of the various boxes marked "go through" which means I got tired of looking at the paper, didn't have time to sort it, and just gave up and boxed it. So tackling one of those boxes has to be on a day when I don't have anything else to do...or not. That day hasn't happened yet, so I just decided to take a slice of time from pending deadlines to look at the waste products from past projects.

I sorted into two piles—keep and throw away. After a while, I became more hardened to what I felt like I could just toss. I threw away memories along with many of my creative efforts. When in doubt, I figured many of the papers were stored on a thumb drive somewhere.

Tossing, sorting, and examining documents was going quite well until I came across Jim's Safe Return application. Then, the world seemed to stand still for just a moment as I recalled filling out the form. That piece of paper was a reality check. If Jim wandered off, he could become lost and need help to be reunited with us.

The part of the document that brought me to tears was the location of his tattoos. I knew one was on his left wrist because he covered it with his watch, one was on his thumb, and another on his shoulder. For some reason, I had trouble remembering just which shoulder was tattooed with his name. I could always picture the tattoo in my mind's eye: "Jim" obviously a homemade tattoo. It looked like a prison tat, but in Jim's case, his cousin Joe did the honors when they were young.

When I first met Jim, I didn't believe he owned a shirt without the sleeves ripped off it. So I saw the tattoo the day I met him, and nearly every day of our marriage. So why did I have this mental glitch about which shoulder?

While fighting the paper war, I found a document that confirmed the tattoo was on his right shoulder. Of course, it was! I'm sure I knew that all along.

Some memories are painful, but I'm thankful that I have them. With all the millions of memories running through 100 billion connectors in my brain, it is no wonder that some of them are hard to find. It might take something to jog that memory and bring it to the forefront. At least that's my story and I'm sticking to it.

With the discovery of the Safe Return application, I decided the paper war was best left on hold for me to return and fight another day. It only goes to show that among all the worthless pieces of paper we hang onto, sometimes a gem exists among them that freshens a memory from a different time and place.

Alzheimer's Future
Research or Palliative Care

I'm a baby boomer and I know just how old we are getting. This year I plan to retire and hope to have time, finally, to enjoy all the activities I've had to put on the back burner or reserve for a few weeks of vacation. What I don't want in my future is to be brought down by Alzheimer's as we know it today.

Alzheimer's disease would rob me of my memories, my skills, and effectively end life as I know it. I want to remain active throughout my old age and still have the ability to enjoy life thoroughly. I want to be like my mother!

We are nearing the crossroads with Alzheimer's as we baby boomers age. Left unchecked, 13.8 million of us can look forward to developing Alzheimer's disease. I don't think there are thirteen of us who want this future, much less 13.8 million.

Why is this important to us? We all want to think that we will be one of the lucky ones without Alzheimer's in our future. The biggest problem is we are not investing in preventing Alzheimer's. We seem to be sitting on our butts instead of doing something about Alzheimer's now.

Do you know how much this country invests in Alzheimer's research? Last year the National Institutes of Health invested $606 million in Alzheimer's research. That seems like a lot of money, doesn't it? In fact, for Alzheimer's it was the first time research funding from NIH exceeded $500 million. Should we be doing a happy dance? Not so fast. How much will it take to find a cure for Alzheimer's? Just to give it some perspective—NIH spends $6 billion a year on cancer, and $3 billion for HIV/AIDS.

I know we have a budgetary crisis, and I really think we need to do something about it. In 2012, the cost of Alzheimer's care totaled $200 billion, including Medicare and Medicaid payments of $140 billion. The cost of Alzheimer's care is expected to increase 500% to $1.1 trillion by 2050 as we baby boomers age.

Think about these staggering numbers for just a moment. I'll admit that I have trouble wrapping my head around numbers that start with a "b," much less a "t". If you look at Alzheimer's from strictly a financial viewpoint, you have to admit that something has to be done. The only logical way to stop this impending financial disaster is to find a cure, or at least treatment that will halt the disease before it destroys independent living.

Are we ever going to accomplish this goal without investing in research? That is a question we need to ask our legislators, and it is one we *do* ask each year during our Capitol Hill visits following the Alzheimer's Advocacy Forum.

For a moment, let's put all talk of financial considerations aside. The bottom line in this entire argument is the emotional impact on those diagnosed with dementia and their families. Alzheimer's is a life-changing event from which there is no turning back. It takes strength and determination to continue with quality life for persons with the disease, their families, and friends.

Though my volunteer work with the Alzheimer's Association, I've met many people with Alzheimer's and caregivers who manage this devastating diagnosis with dignity and courage. They have allowed news media into their homes to bring awareness. They don purple sashes, talk to their legislators about the disease, and leave a sense of urgency in their wake. Advocates with the disease give a face to the 5.4 million Americans who are living with Alzheimer's right now, right here, in the United States.

So when we talk about the future of Alzheimer's, we need to push, and push hard, for a cure, not palliative care, for 5.4 million people today or 13.8 million in 2050. Each life disrupted by Alzheimer's is one too many. Our loved ones are not statistics—they are human beings with families that love them and memories far too precious to lose.

Thundersnow

We knew the storm was coming and needed to plan accordingly. Although the amount of snow on the ground was deceptively light at 6:40 a.m., the time I usually leave for work, the forecast warned that this was just the beginning of a long day. I stayed home deciding I'd rather be snowed in than out. Having been caught in both situations, on my last year in the working world, I have no desire to put my car in a ditch.

I do believe the nearly foot of snow was more than expected. Snow fell at about an inch an hour, and to make it more interesting, thunder rumbled. The thundersnow fell, fell, and fell. I started measuring with a ruler, and the last time I sank it into the ground, a mere inch showed. Then it started sleeting.

The intense snowfall brought the world to a screeching halt as banks, shopping centers, restaurants, and other businesses sent employees home. Interstates and airports closed. So many cars were stranded that in Kansas City, they towed them off by the hundreds in order to clear the highways.

Thundersnow is rare, and a little bit weird. In a normal thunderstorm with rain, thunder can be heard for many miles from where the lightning strikes. Snow acts as an acoustic suppresser and the sound of thunder can only be heard for two to three miles.

When we wake up each morning, we expect the usual, and we can be caught off guard when the unusual happens. The unexpected can strike at any point in time. It can come in the form of a phone call, a text message, a medical test, a bulletin on TV, or a knock on the door.

Hundreds of mundane days can be shattered with one nanosecond of the unusual. We can often chunk our lives into sections based on moments when our world tilted and never quite righted itself. One of those times in my life was when the doctor told us Jim had "dementia of the Alzheimer's type."

When you hear news like that, your ears start to buzz, as if they can't bear to hear the unexpected information. Your heart quickens, and you stop breathing as your brain echoes with the words it refuses to process. Denial, hope, and despair wage a battle to see which one can get the upper hand.

Jim always said, "I don't have *that*." He preferred to think the psychiatrist was inept. It turned out that Jim had a rare type of dementia. It wasn't Alzheimer's, but it was just as bad, with the same inevitable outcome.

Not a day passes in this world without someone struggling to live through an impossible situation. Globally, 156,000 people die each day. That is a lot of grief to go around. In order to live a happy, normal life, we often harden ourselves to suffering if it does not personally affect us.

On the flip side of the death card, we celebrate the births of 350,000 babies each day. Of course, some people have more cause to celebrate births than others do. Babies born into poverty, although loved, may be a worry to his or her parents who struggle to provide basic food and shelter. Through the joy, every parent is afraid that something will go wrong. Our instinct is to protect our children from the cruelties of the world, but that is a goal set up to fail. Too little protection puts them in danger, too much can make them vulnerable. Births and deaths while unusual in our personal lives are daily occurrences when we look outside ourselves.

What does the future hold? No one knows. The future is both as unpredictable and predictable as the weather. Weather is never an exact science. Yes, sometimes we can be warned of the possibilities, or probabilities, but what will really happen can be a different story.

This morning I saw two opposing predictions for the storm expected on Sunday. We can have another ten inches of snow, or a thunderstorm with rain. In either case, it is expected to come in the night, so it's anyone's guess as to what Monday will bring. Will it be a normal workday, or another weird day with thundersnow?

Worrywartitis and a Storm Called Rocky

I tend to be a worrywart and when I heard the predictions last Monday, it was all I could do to keep from freaking out. We had just weathered a storm that dumped a foot of snow on us and then the models were calling for another six to twenty-two inches with thirty-mile-an-hour winds. I kept telling myself they could be wrong.

No amount of self-reassurance could keep me from worrying. I was awake more than asleep on Monday night as the storm raged. My cell phone said "light snow" but the wind-driven snow was anything but light.

By morning, I knew I'd be foolish to head out to work in the storm. Monday evening, we arranged to have some of the office staff picked up and taken to work. It was a good thing because we had major power outages at the electric cooperative where I work.

I was able to make some phone calls from home to help a little, but the brunt of the work fell on other staff, and, of course, the linemen who braved the blizzard to restore power to the people sitting in cold, dark homes.

As the storm named Rocky raged on, we became more aware of the damage. Nearly two-thirds of our system was in the dark.

I made it to work on Wednesday, and the rest of the week was a blur of calls and stories of how people coped without power—some of them for four days. The calls ranged from one extreme to the other—pleasant understanding to unbridled anger. The longer the outage lasted, the more exhausted our employees were and the more frustrated the members became.

Many conversations stuck with me, but I think the one that hit home the hardest was the lady talking about an elderly couple who were staying in town. They wanted to go home. She said, "He has serious health problems and didn't bring enough medication. She gets so upset when things don't go right. You know how people can get."

"I certainly do," I said. "I'm the same way. When something doesn't go right, I get upset."

The tension was broken as we shared a laugh about human nature.

Throughout the week, I thought of the message Pastor Jim gave on Sunday. He said fear has many names and one of them is worry. I'm not sure where he got the statistics he quoted, but they made perfect sense to me.

Jim Downing said that forty percent of what we worry about never happens. I would say looking back at what I worry about, that's probably a little low for me. But then, I'm a worrywart so it stands to reason that my personal fruitless worrying would be higher than average.

Thirty percent of worrying is about the past and can't be changed. I saw an example of that when one of the employees asked me if she could take off next Monday. She needed to watch her grandchild, but she was afraid that she would be needed at work. I put it on the calendar and told her, "Sometimes family just has to come first. It took me a long time to realize that and I missed a lot of events because I put work first." With tears in her eyes, she relayed a story of when she put work first and had never stopped regretting it.

Twelve percent is over criticism. I used to get my feelings hurt easily, but I outgrew that. I think to overcome worry about what others think of me, I've acknowledged that I'm not perfect and some people cannot be satisfied. I can't do much about those who criticize me, but I can either use the criticism to improve myself, or if it's unwarranted, let it die. I learned a lot about criticism this week.

Ten percent of worry is over health—yours or a loved one's. I think we worry more about our loved ones that ourselves. One time I needed surgery and Jim kept insisting I tell my mother. I wanted to tell her when it was over. He couldn't handle the stress on his own and he called her! I know that Jim's dementia worried me more than it did him.

Eight percent of our worries are about real problems. Sometimes, worry can be a positive thing because we prepare ourselves. Some of those who worried about the storm used their concern as a springboard to prepare. They arranged a place to stay; they fired up generators or wood stoves. They became ingenious and went into survivor mode. Sure, they were as inconvenienced as anyone else was, but they found a way to make the best of a bad situation. One woman fired up her grill to melt snow water to flush her toilet.

I wish I could say knowing the statistics means I'm now worry free, but it doesn't. As long as snowstorms are wicked enough to have names, many of us will worry. Action does help alleviate some of the worry, along with faith and trust in a higher power.

Spring Forward

Tonight, or should I say early tomorrow morning, is the time to set our clocks for daylight saving time. We know which direction to change the clock by reminding each other to "spring forward."

So, I don't have a problem with springing forward, but changing time, doesn't work for me. But then, I don't have any choice in the matter. I can't continue using standard time when the rest of the country sets their clocks forward. Heck, it's hard enough for me to be on time under the best of circumstances.

When the time changes, it takes weeks before my biological clock gets back in sync with the clock on the wall. Anytime I travel to a different time zone, I go through this big mental adjustment. Whether I travel east or west doesn't seem to make much difference. Either one will throw me for a loop, either while I'm there or when I get home.

One year, I carefully entered a schedule into my cell phone for the Alzheimer's Advocacy Forum in Washington, D.C. I'm probably the only person who ever went to that much trouble, just to realize that I somehow managed to have the schedule set to Central time and every event I had painstakingly entered did not switch to the new time zone. Sure, the phone changed, but the entries did not change with it.

It seems that as I get older, I've reverted to questioning things—like daylight saving time. The first thing I found when I Googled the time change was that it is not "daylight savings time," it is "daylight saving time." In all honesty, we have the exact same number of daylight hours no matter what time the clock says. The whole idea is to rearrange time to suit our lifestyle, not to save any time whatsoever. Rearranging time is, of course, the biggest advantage.

The downside is that it messes up some of us for days, if not weeks. On the Monday following the time change, more auto accidents occur. Work productivity suffers.

I remember many years ago when I worked at a different job, we noticed one employee did not show up to work the day after the time change. One of my co-workers called him and asked what he was doing.

"Drinking coffee," the missing employee replied, "like I always do this time of day." Boy, was he ever surprised to find out he was sitting there drinking coffee when he was expected to be at work.

Regardless of the extra daylight hours at the end of the workday, I always feel like an hour of my life has gone missing. It usually means an hour less of sleep for me since I can't seem to go to bed early enough to get a full night's sleep under the best circumstances.

The older I get, the harder it is to make any fast moves and springing sounds like it could be beyond my speed. So, if springing is too hard, we could simply move forward. Each year we can move forward just a little slower.

Technically, it is not yet spring although the rain last night and the sound of dripping snow were hopeful signs of impending spring weather. All I know is that this is one year that proved that silly groundhog was wrong in his prediction—really, really wrong.

Before long, it will be officially springtime. Maybe by then, I'll forgive Punxsutawney Phil for his *faux pas*. By summer, I'll have adjusted to the time change and can enjoy the extra hour of evening daylight, which is after all the advantage of daylight saving time.

Dreams and Lewy Body Disease

I've always been a dreamer and often awaken in the night puzzling over what remote area of my brain produced those mini-motion pictures. My dreams are often a mystery, especially when I wake up with vivid images of my nighttime adventures.

We all dream, but some people cannot remember their dreams when they awaken. I tend to remember mine and find myself inspired, disturbed, or downright puzzled. I kept a dream journal for a long time as a means to jumpstart my writing. I am amazed at how many ideas I can glean from my dreams.

Just a few of the images I remember from last night: (1) I dreamed my house was connected to my work and a former employee had removed my cat's litter box and let her outside. (2) I had gone to the dentist (whose office was at a mall) and forgot to remove the clothing protector when I left, but managed to accidentally put on two fancy scarves that didn't belong to me. (3) My sister and I hopped on a trolley to return to the mall to get my coat and return the scarves.

Does any of that make sense? In a strange way, most of it does relate vaguely to something that happened the day before. Think about Dorothy and the *Wizard of Oz*. Her dream from the bump to her head was a fascinating distortion of the events leading up to the tornado.

Did you know that studies before 1950 showed that most people dreamed in black and white? That began to change during the sixties, and now about eighty-eight percent of us dream in color. Nearly ninety-six percent younger than twenty-five dream in color. This change is believed to be the result of the changeover from black and white film to color media. It really makes sense if you think about it.

One of the theories behind dreaming is that dreams are our way of consolidating our memories and attempting to make sense of them. We dream during the REM (rapid eye movement) stage. While our eyes move, normally, the rest of our body is paralyzed. In our family, several of us have, or have had, paralyzing nightmares. During this event, we are trying to wake from a bad dream and realize that although the mind is awake, the body cannot move. It is a disconcerting feeling, to say the least.

On CBS This Morning, Dr. James Galvin talked about a study from Mayo Clinic about dreams and the connection to dementia. This study showed that if you act out your dreams by kicking, shouting, punching, or thrashing about, you are at higher risk of developing dementia.

In fact, the study shows this is the strongest predictor of developing Lewy Body disease.

Approximately 1.3 million people in the United States have Lewy Body disease. Both men and women develop the disease, but it is more common in men. Lewy Body disease is under-diagnosed because of symptoms it shares with Alzheimer's and Parkinson's, but subtle differences can help physicians make a diagnosis. Now, added to other differences, acting out dreams may be another indicator of the disease.

Lewy Body disease is best treated with a comprehensive approach by a team of specialists. Cholinesterase inhibitors, such as Aricept, work well on Lewy Body disease. In fact, it is believed the cholinesterase inhibitors are more effective on this disease than on Alzheimer's. The movement disorders associated with Lewy Body is treated with Parkinson's medication. Antipsychotic drugs should not be used to treat hallucinations because they affect persons with Lewy Body disease differently. These drugs worsen symptoms in fifty percent of those using them, and can cause a fatal reaction called neuroleptic malignant syndrome (NMS).

Of course, one of the problems with Lewy Body disease is REM Sleep Behavior Disorder. This is often treated with melatonin or clonazepam.

It is important to remember that if you move around and act out your dreams, it does not mean that you have Lewy Body disease or that you will develop it. If you develop signs of dementia, it is something to mention to your team of physicians during testing to determine the cause of your cognitive problems.

The connection between sleep and function the following day is strong. A lack of sleep or disturbed sleep affects our thinking process. Now, acting out during sleep means a person is five times more likely to develop Lewy Body dementia than those who sleep quietly during dreams.

Sleep is essential to our health and wellbeing. The REM stage of sleep is when our minds can take us places we will only reach through dreams.

What's in a Name?

At Easter services, we enjoyed a parade of banners bearing different names for Jesus. If you think about it, many names are used in the Bible...Lord, Redeemer, Savior, Christ, The Word, Alpha and Omega...just to name a few.

During the sermon, Pastor Jim mentioned that according to the census, the most common women's names are Mary, Patricia, and Linda. I really didn't need the census to know Linda is a common name, especially for those of us born in the Fifties and early Sixties. I went to a small school and throughout all my school years, our class had five girls named Linda. One year, to avoid confusion, the teacher called all five of us by our middle names.

"Why did you name me Linda?" I asked my mom.

"Because it's such a beautiful name, and I never knew anyone named Linda," she said. Well, there must have been a lot of mommas with the same mindset.

If there was one thing I hated worse than my first name, it was my middle name. That probably came from my brothers making fun of my middle name, Sue, since it sounded similar to how the hogs were called. I'm not kidding about that.

I have a friend that I've known for forty years that calls me Linda Lou. The funny thing is that I'm positive he really thinks that is my name. I've never told him any different, and now his wife calls me Linda Lou.

"Why didn't you name me Ellen?" I asked my mom—many, many times. I wouldn't have even minded Linda Ellen because I would have used my middle name for sure. My mom and grandmother shared the middle name Ellen, and I loved that name. I envied that name. Neither of them used it anymore than I used my middle name.

They say a rose by any other name would smell just as sweet, but when it comes to human nature, our names can have an effect on our lives. Johnny Cash sang a song about a "Boy Named Sue" and the hardships on a boy growing up with a girl's name. Of course, his dad named him Sue so that he would grow up tough. And, at least in the song, the name choice made a difference.

Some people's names are immortalized when a disease is named after them, including several that affect the brain. Alzheimer's is named after Alois Alzheimer who discovered the plaques and tangles that are the hallmarks of the disease. Another dementia, Pick's disease is named after Arnold Pick, a professor of psychiatry from Prague, who first described the disease. Lewy Body dementia is named after a German scientist Friederich Lewy, who studied at the Alois Alzheimer's laboratory in Munich. Hans Creutzfieldt and Alfons Jakob studied at the same laboratory during the time Pick was there. They, of course, were the first to describe Creutzfeldt-Jakob disease, which is so hard to pronounce that it is known as CJD or "mad cow disease." Down's syndrome is named after John Landon Down. About 25% or more of individuals with Down's syndrome will develop Alzheimer's after the age of thirty-five.

Most of us will never have anything named after us, other than maybe our descendents. You never hear of any babies named Linda anymore. In fact, if you wanted a girl born this year to have a name different from her classmates, you would be safe with Linda. I'm thinking that by the time we have great-grandchildren the name will make a comeback. It will be such an old name that it will come back in style.

My name was common, and I didn't have to worry about people misspelling or mispronouncing it. When you see some of the unusual names, with unusual spellings, pronunciation can have your tongue turned upside down. What does that do to a person's psyche to have their name pronounced wrong by every stranger they meet?

What about people who have names so silly that they are taunted by other children? Sometimes you wonder what people were thinking when they named a defenseless child something so ridiculous.

Names of places, people, and things can immediately create mental images in our minds. Whether a name is unusual or common, it identifies you to those who know you. When your family and friends hear your name, they immediately make a connection to the unique and special person you are.

April Rain, Storms, and Hopeful Sunshine

April is a kaleidoscope month with beautiful patterns and disturbing images. Rain and clouds bring sad thoughts. Storms can light the skies and simultaneously startle us with heart stopping thunder, wind, hail, and tornadoes. Along with spring comes a period of renewed hope when dazzling sunshine warms the ground and flowers, mushrooms, and foliage cover the earth with a lush blanket of beauty.

April is a month of memories for me. It was on a hot day in April when Jim left his body behind and went to a place where he could be whole again. April rain falls in my heart when I allow myself to remember those days of April when he was ready to leave, but I wasn't ready to let go.

Perhaps, in lieu of sad thoughts I've packed April with activities. This month is full of conferences, meetings, and my annual trip to Washington, D.C., to advocate for Alzheimer's.

Saturday, I drove to Kansas City for an inspirational breakfast and spent the morning with some amazing women. We each introduced ourselves and talked about our first job and the most innovative thing in our first workplace. We shared laughter and memories of those jobs and discussed how far the business world has advanced over the years.

Was it talking of old times that turned my thoughts to the past? Or was it just that this is April? The rush of memories expressed themselves with April rain flowing from my eyes and I made the decision to stop at the cemetery on my way home.

I pulled off the interstate when I saw the sign for the Missouri Veterans Cemetery at Higginsville. I stopped at Walmart hoping to find some flowers and instead settled for a colorful plant in a pot decorated with two birds facing each other. As I left Walmart, I drove through McDonald's and bought a cheeseburger and fries.

A few miles out of town, I pulled through the gate into the cemetery and drove to the columbarium. I had the peaceful, quiet cemetery all to myself.

I shared my water with the plant and placed it beneath Jim's memorial. I sat on a bench and ate my lunch while I reflected on our life together. Jim would have looked forward to my impending retirement and trips to see family and friends. He would have wanted to spend time animal watching in the Rocky Mountains he had grown to love so much. He would have been so proud of our children and grandchildren. He would have loved showing the grandkids his childhood places and sharing his stories and memories. That was what made Jim, Jim. We would have spent time having those soul-searching conversations about life, death, and the time between. Time. We ran out of it.

I sat on the bench reminiscing when I heard a sound behind me, breaking the silence. I turned to see…nothing but the committal shelter, with the flags flying high in front of it. I heard the noise again and realized it was the flags flapping in the breeze.

Jim's physical presence has been gone for eight years. Not a day goes by without thoughts of Jim. He is imprinted on my heart where he'll always share a part of my being. Was he perfect? No. But in many ways, he was perfect for me, and we seemed to complete each other.

After my time alone with Jim and our memories, I drove away. The tears vanished, and I thought about how fortunate my life has been. I've learned to be independent and comfortable in my skin. Loneliness and sadness visit only occasionally—as unexpected and quick as the lightening of an April storm.

I have lived a full and rich life that began on a December day in Hawaii when I married Jim. Our time together began on an April day when he returned from Vietnam and ended on another April day thirty-five years later.

Our time together ended, but life goes on for me. I plan to enjoy many years of fun, laughter, and joy. Family and friends are the essence of life, and they provide circles of love without beginning or end.

Advocates and Avocados

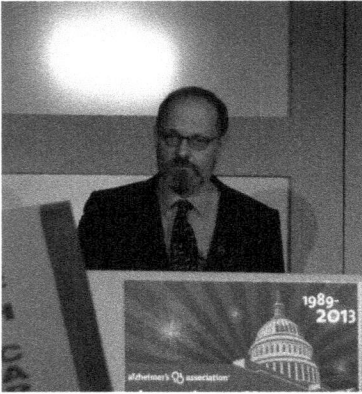

David Hyde Pierce, a champion for Alzheimer's, began this year's forum by joking about how the word advocate in Spanish is *abogado*, which sounds like "avocado." It was his observation that "Avocadoes are like Alzheimer's advocates because they are irresistible, and they have big nuts." About Alzheimer's disease, David said, "It's not going to stop until we stop it." Then, the most unusual call to action I've heard in the thirteen forums I've attended, "Avacados, let's roll!"

Of course, we all laughed at David Hyde Pierce's jokes because, let's face it, he knows how to deliver a punch line. Jokes aside, just like us, he is here on a mission—flying back and forth from New York to take part in this forum. Because, like the more than nine hundred advocates packed into the large ballroom, he has a personal stake in finding a cure for this disease. He's met Alzheimer's and knows what a cruel disease it is.

The conference, as usual, was a whirlwind of activities. Dr. Collins, director of National Institutes of Health, announced that in a unique step, NIH has designated $40 million of its 2013 budget for Alzheimer's. In addition, an indication of the nation's attention to the underfunded Alzheimer's research funds, the president's 2014 budget allocates $80 million to research.

Glen Campbell joined us for the National Alzheimer's Dinner. He entered the room a few feet from me, but I couldn't get my camera turned on in time to get a picture.

After dinner, I managed to work my way to the front of the crowd to get a picture of him and my mom. More important than the photo ops was the presentation of the Sargent and Eunice Shriver Profiles in Courage Award to Glen Campbell and his family. The "Rhinestone Cowboy" strode to the stage and accepted his award with humility that belied his outer showmanship.

After several other deserving awards, the Outstanding Advocate of the Year Award was presented to Dr. Ron Grant who has early onset Alzheimer's. He thanked God and the Oklahoma-Arkansas Chapter for giving him the courage to face the disease. He said, "We live in the greatest nation on the planet, but I have to ask—in such a great nation, how many more families are going to have to suffer the devastation of this disease?" Grant concluded with a break in his voice, "How many more of us are going to have to die before we stand up and say enough?"

That, I would say, is the most important question of the entire forum. How many precious lives have been lost to the costliest disease in the United States? Officially, 83,437 died from Alzheimer's in 2010. Other health conditions are often listed as the cause of death although Alzheimer's causes the other condition.

In 2013, an estimated 450,000 will die *with* Alzheimer's.

We ended the conference part of the forum armed with statistics and tactics, but the most important element of our visits to the hill would be the power of our personal stories. As this *abogado* "avocado" prepared to charge the hill, I left the room with Dr. Grant's haunting question echoing in my brain, "how many?"

The Expected Unexpected

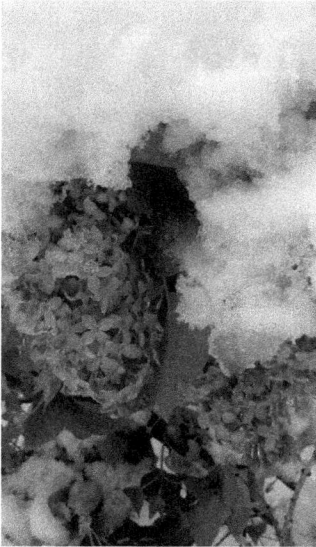

Winter stretched into spring and blew in with a vengeance in March. April came, and we breathed a sigh of relief, although spring was late coming. Earlier in the week, I noticed that my lilacs had finally bloomed and filled the air with their distinctive scent. May apples formed umbrellas and Missourians took to the woods in search of morel mushrooms.

May came with seventy-degree weather. Then, this morning the unexpected happened, and I woke up to snow. Seriously? Snow in May? Yes, I know, snow had been predicted, but I figured we might have some white flakes mixed in with rain, but it would melt as soon as it hit the ground. Instead, it snowed for several hours and the ground was piled with puffy white snow more befitting a winter day—not a May day.

Through my patio door, I could see green leaves covered with snow. It almost looked surreal. I can't recall ever seeing Mother Nature so confused. I could see how a heating/cooling system could wear out trying to keep up with the drastic changes in temperature. A forty-degree variance in one week takes a lot of getting used to.

The unexpected weather made me think about other unexpected events in my life. Jim's dementia was unexpected. He was so young that it took more than a year before dementia was diagnosed. Even after I learned everything I could about the disease, the change, though expected, was still unexpected. It didn't seem possible that the man I knew could be consumed by a disease that erased memories and skills built over a lifetime.

Then, the expected outcome hit with unexpected emotions. It didn't matter that I knew the disease was going to progress and take on a life of its own. A point came when our world changed, we changed too. We adapted and kept on going—taking one day at a time, or sometimes an hour at a time. Life became the peaks and valleys of human nature.

Being a primary caregiver for someone with dementia is challenging. Caregiving requires a talent for thinking on your feet, and developing an ability to expect the unexpected at all times. There is no way to sugarcoat it and say that you will always be at the top of your game. After all, the best caregiver in the world is only human. Even good caregivers make mistakes, have regrets, and may suffer from serious doubts that they can do this job day after day, year after year.

Have you ever noticed that sometimes the most difficult days in our lives are the ones that define us? When you face challenges and give it your best, you develop strength and self-assurance you will never get by running away. When you look at the positive, and seek out small moments of joy, your life can take on new purpose.

After the snow quit this morning, I walked out into the yard to have a look around. As I looked back across the yard, I could see my footprints in the snow, wandering here and there, but clearly showing where I had been as I searched for the unexpected on this strange day in May. Then, I spotted my lilacs, peeking out beneath a layer of glistening, pristine snow. It was like finding a promise of better days ahead.

Friends Indeed

For some reason the phrase, "A friend in need is a friend indeed" has been on my mind all week. Odd, that a saying I cannot recall ever using in my life should be echoing through my brain nonstop.

I suppose many things could have triggered this thought. It could have been the news story of three women who forged a bond during a decade of captivity. Or it could have been the finalists on American Idol who seemed to value friendship over winning the title. Although, my DVR kicked off during the final moments, I later saw a picture of a frozen moment of time—Kree, with a look of pure joy, turned toward a stunned Candace. Maybe part of it could be tuning in to re-runs of *Golden Girls* and seeing the interaction between Blanche, Rose, and Dorothy— friends who fuss, fight, banter, and insult each other but still love each other.

These fascinating events could have been the impetus behind my obsession about the nuances of friendship, but I think it was more personal than that. I have been blessed with the gift of abundant friendship from some truly amazing men and women. My friendship list, and not just the one on Facebook, reads like the *Who's Who of Friends Indeed*.

My first friends are made up of family and co-workers. Over the past fifteen years, I've greatly widened my circle of friends by giving time to groups, clubs, and organizations. I've become friends with like-minded people I would never have met otherwise.

Although, I would love to honor all my friends, I've decided to limit it to one handsome southern gentleman and three women I met during my first Alzheimer's advocacy visit to Washington, D.C.

Ralph and I were party crashers at a reception for executive directors. We were board members who had come to the forum and didn't know anyone besides the executive directors of our chapters. He and I wound up exploring the Capital city and became fast friends. Ralph declared himself to be the oldest advocate, but he knew he had to do everything he could for his lovely wife.

In the first plenary session, a woman with smooth brown hair framing her face stood up to talk about her husband who had early onset Alzheimer's. She echoed my own concerns that not enough was being done to find a cure, and that if one came, it was probably going to be too late. I understood her pain and heartbreak. When the session ended, I made my way through the crowd of people and introduced myself to Jane. It was like finding a long lost friend.

Later that first year, I met two more women, Kathy and Sarah. Kathy had a winning smile and flashing eyes. Sarah, slim and trim, was beautiful inside and out. We four women, plus Ralph, became inseparable. We had the bond of being caregivers for spouses with Alzheimer's, and after sharing the heartbreak and sadness, we often regaled each other with humorous stories. The one thing we all had in common was a wacky sense of humor.

Just like in the movies, we met at the same place, same time each year at the forum. Sometimes we shared a few emails between, but it seemed as if the forum was our special time, our sister/brotherhood time. Each year was a reunion of heart friends.

Jane and I roomed together a few times. In our down time, we spent time people watching and making up stories about them. "See that woman in the slinky dress and high heels? She's on her way to meet a lover." Another year, we stood watch over the building across the street that had suspicious activity every night. Big limos parked in front of it and random lights came on in offices. "Spies!" we decided. We spent so much time together that some people thought I was from New York too. When the New York group bought tickets to a play at Ford's Theatre, Jane insisted they buy one for her roommate.

Time passed and our reunions were sobered by death as we lost our spouses, one by one. Then one year Jane didn't come. A few years later, Ralph didn't come. Now Kathy, Sarah, and I meet each year with hugs, laughter, and tears. They each hold a special place in my heart, and I am so thankful to know them. We are friends indeed and our love for each other surpasses the bounds of time and distance.

Caregiver Emotion #1 – Guilt

Recently, I read an article on caregiver emotions, and thought the idea worth expanding on. Having been a caregiver for ten years, I was familiar with all the emotions featured in the article, as well as several others.

Emotions can run high for caregivers, and I suppose that if you asked what a caregiver was feeling, guilt could easily be at the top of the list. Even good caregivers feel guilt no matter how unfounded. Some of us just have this little guilt complex that travels rampantly throughout our brains.

I don't know about you, but I can manage to feel guilty over trivial matters. Some of the guilt associated with caregivers can be circumstances that seem entirely beyond our control. One of the guilt generators can be how a caregiver can be pulled in several different directions at one time. I think this is especially true when the person with dementia is young. I know that I was conflicted with work and my responsibility to care for Jim. Since I was only in my mid-forties when Jim began to need someone to watch over him, I didn't think that quitting my job was an option. That is not the decision every caregiver makes, and I could see where both options could cause some feelings of guilt.

Had I taken a leave of absence, it would have lasted for several years because Alzheimer's develops over time and can last for ten to twenty years. There were several advantages to keeping my job, one of which was to keep my health insurance. With good insurance, we were able to afford the diagnostic tests necessary to determine the type of disease and scope of the damage to Jim's brain. The insurance meant we could afford the expensive medication. I was also able to continue making a living that paid the bills and avoided the stress and strain involved with having to make hard choices of medical care or paying the electric bill. Another advantage of working is that although Jim was never off my mind, I did have something apart from caregiving to fill my days. I was able to interact with other people at a time when Jim became silent and no longer carried on a conversation.

The downside was that I scrambled to find someone to watch him during the day. Between family, professional caregivers, my day off each week, and vacation, we managed to have someone with him at all times. It wasn't easy, and had it not been for a flexible work schedule, it would have been an impossible situation. I still managed to feel guilty at times because I wasn't there for him when he needed me, but in retrospect, I think it was the right decision for me.

Still, since I used all the caregivers during the workday, it meant that nights and weekends were my turn. Sometimes, Jim would be stubborn and uncooperative, and occasionally, I would lose patience. I beat myself up for those times when I blamed him rather than the disease. One time, I yelled at him and just about the time I felt totally like a worm, he started laughing at me over the colorful language I had used. We wound up having a good laugh over it, and it makes a happy memory rather than a guilt-ridden moment.

I think one of the most common reasons caregivers feel guilt is the nursing home decision. No matter how necessary, or thoughtful, the decision, it tends to make a caregiver feel that she has let down the person she loves. It is especially difficult when the family has promised they will never put their loved one in a nursing home. Caregivers feel as if they have broken a promise when making the only decision that makes sense in the situation.

The nursing home decision was one I struggled with and put off as long as possible. Jim only slept a few hours a night, and I was constantly exhausted. He began to wander off, and no matter how careful we were, it only took a split second for him to disappear. It finally got to the point that we needed to put him in a safe place before he wandered off and we couldn't find him. In that case, there would be no nursing home decision necessary. In my opinion, that wasn't an option.

Unbridled guilt isn't good for anyone. To help take control of your attitude, you need to have a reality check. If you are doing your best as a caregiver, and as a person, that is all you can do. There is a huge gap between reality and perfection. You don't need to be the best caregiver in the world; you just need to be the best caregiver you can be. In the end, you need to make tough decisions that are not only best for your loved one, but also for you, the caregiver.

Caregiver Emotion #2 – Resentment

Resentment is an emotion you may not want to admit you have. You usually try to keep it at bay and not let it define the kind of person you are. Yet, for Alzheimer's caregivers, it is hard not to feel resentment from time-to-time.

Resentment comes in many forms. You may resent other family members if you don't think they are pulling their weight. Or, you may resent a family member who seems to take over and not listen to your ideas or opinions. In turn, if you are not the caregiver, she may resent you for not supporting her, or second guessing her, when she is making tough decisions.

At times, you may find that you even resent your loved one for not cooperating when you are trying to help. I know that when I tried to take Jim to daycare, he would balk and refuse to go most of the time. I wanted him to go to daycare so that I could keep him at home longer rather than make the nursing home decision. He didn't understand that—he just knew he wanted to stay at home.

Resentment can build because life just seems to be out of control. All your well-laid plans go awry, and there isn't a darn thing you can do to make life normal again. In the case of early onset, you may have been looking forward to retirement just to see your retirement dreams vanish. Instead of travel and relaxation, you are a full-time caregiver taking on an overwhelming job.

One thing is for sure—if you are consumed with resentment, you need to find a way to overcome this self-destructive emotion before it turns into anger. Have you ever thought that when you are resentful, it is such an internal emotion that you are often the only person affected?

Okay, now that you've identified an emotion you want no part of, what can you do? Think about the things that make you resentful, and seek a solution for each one. If you are feeling that you are doing much more than your share, ask for help. Often family members don't realize that you need help. You may seem so confident and capable, that they feel inadequate to attempt taking your place even for a short time.

If you're resentful of your loved one's behavior, just remember that the disease causes the behavior and your loved one is not just being willful. I always knew that Jim's behavior was something he couldn't help. Don't get me wrong, he was always stubborn, but not unreasonable. No one can overcome the effects of damaged brain cells. My mom always said, "If a person has a broken leg, no one expects him to walk on that leg." Her point was that Alzheimer's was much more of a physical problem than a broken leg, and no one could expect Jim to think the same with a diseased brain as he did with a healthy one.

I coped with the resentment of having no control over the progression of the disease by focusing on what I could do. I could see that Jim had all the tests to determine he did not have an irreversible condition, and that he had the best treatment options available. Then, I volunteered for the Alzheimer's Association because it provided a positive experience for me. It helped *me* to know that I could help raise funds for the Alzheimer's Association support and services to benefit other caregivers. I became an advocate so I could educate legislators on both the state and national level on the urgency of funding effective treatments for Alzheimer's, or better yet, a cure.

Resentment may be a feeling you want to hide, but it *is* a normal, human emotion. Just like all negative emotions, it can damage your physical and emotional health, or you can use it to make yourself stronger. Coping with resentment, can make you more assertive, in a good way, and that can help you be a better caregiver, which in turn, helps your loved one's quality of life.

Caregiver Emotion #3 – Anger

When you are a caregiver for a loved one with a serious health problem like Alzheimer's, you might find that you need anger management classes. Of course, you are going to be so busy with day-to-day duties that you aren't going to have time for any additional activities.

What does it take to push your buttons and make you see red? Something that normally doesn't bother you can trigger a rise in blood pressure when you are emotionally vulnerable. It is important to learn to recognize and address the issues that cause you to react with anger, especially if you are angry with your loved one.

The characteristics of Alzheimer's can grate on the caregiver's nerves. Repetitive behavior can be distressing to the caregiver. One of the early symptoms of Alzheimer's is loss of short-term memory that causes your loved one to forget they already asked you a question and that you answered them. It will do no good to point out that you already answered and to let your irritation turn into anger. It is better to answer the question again.

Be aware that although your loved one might be asking you one question, due to failing communication skills, he may actually intend to ask a different question. Be vigilant to make sure your loved one's needs are being met. Often, you can distract or redirect your loved one.

Pacing is another repetitive behavior that can bother a caregiver. Jim used to pace through the house constantly. The bad thing was that the minute I was distracted, he would pace right out the door and down the gravel road. He would never turn around and come back, so I would have to get in the car and go after him. After about five or six trips to pick him up, I would find that I was seething. Sometimes, it helped if I just went for a walk with him. Although, he might take off again given a chance, at least the walks were a good stress reliever for me!

Another thing that can anger a caregiver is unfair criticism of how you are caring for your loved one, especially from someone who isn't helping. You may not feel like explaining every situation, but until someone has been a primary caregiver for a person with Alzheimer's, they can't comprehend what it's like to walk in your shoes.

You may be angry at the disease that is taking your loved one away. Alzheimer's has no cure and treatment only addresses the symptoms. To help assuage my anger at the disease, I became an Alzheimer's volunteer. The Walk to End Alzheimer's was a way to help the Chapter provide support and services for families coping with dementia. I became an advocate to add my voice in support of research to find a cure. By helping others, I helped myself more.

You can't predict every situation that is going to make you angry, but you can alleviate some of the tension by taking a step back before you react. You don't have to count to ten but take a few deep breaths and think before you do or say something you will regret.

Humor helps tremendously. If you can see the humor in the situation, it may keep you from ever being angry in the first place. As long as your anger causes no harm to your loved one, you can also see the humor in that.

Occasional anger is a normal emotion, and as long as you control your anger and not let it control you, it should not affect your ability to be a calm, patient caregiver. Of course, regularly taking a break from caregiving helps your mood and energizes you to continue providing a loving and safe environment for your loved one.

Caregiver Emotion #4 – Worry

Jim used to say I was a worrywart, and I can't deny that it was (and still is) true. At one time, I remember telling him, "I have to worry, because you don't."

When we were first married, I worried about money because we never seemed to have too much of it. Paying bills on time and not racking up debt was important to me. I also felt a need for the safety net of putting a little aside for unexpected expenses. Although I was always conscious of our financial situation, one time I made an error in my checkbook. The bank didn't return the check, but notified me that I needed more money in my account. We had money in another account, but I was worried because I received the notice on a weekend and the bank was closed.

It so happened that Jim was in the hospital in the stress unit and his mom and dad didn't want me to tell him about the problem with the bank. The minute Jim saw my face, he demanded to know what was wrong. When I told him, he said, "Honey, when a problem can be solved by throwing a little money at it, it just isn't worth worrying about." Those were wise words, indeed.

Unfortunately, many of the worries you have as a caregiver cannot be solved with money. Being a caregiver is demanding, and requires a lot of patience. You might worry that you don't have the qualities you need to take care of your loved one. Sometimes a bigger worry is that if your loved one is being cared for by someone else, substitute caregivers may not meet all of his needs. You worry that your loved one feels abandoned or is lonely and afraid.

You can even worry about worrying! It can become an endless cycle of worry that puts gray hair on your head, or worse, causes other health problems.

What can you do to break the cycle? I've found a few good diversions that help me keep worry under control. First, stay active and busy. This will give you something else to think about other than the problem that is worrying you.

Second, look for solutions. Instead of worrying for the sake of worrying, calm down and think about ways to lessen your anxiety. I worried about Jim falling when he was in the nursing home. He was trying to get up in the mornings before the aides came to help him out of bed, and they were finding him on the floor. Jim had always been an early riser, so I suggested they wake him up about five in the morning and help him out of bed. Problem solved.

Third, share your worries with friends, family members, a support group, or a therapist. When you share your worries, it accomplishes a couple of things. Talking about it can result in thinking out loud, and you might be able to find a solution or at least come to grips with your emotional dilemma. Other people may suggest ideas that you never considered.

Many of the big problems in life that fill our days and nights with worry cannot be resolved, and with those problems, you will need to find methods that help you manage your worry. It may be as complex as regular visits to a therapist, or as simple as reading a good book at bedtime to take your mind off your worries so you can go to sleep. The important thing is to find what works for *you.*

Caregiver Emotion #5—Loneliness

Before I even knew Sarah Harris, her words in the national Alzheimer's newsletter resonated with me. When she spoke at the candlelight vigil many years ago, she said, "Alzheimer's is a lonely disease."

Dementia disrupts personal relationships in a way that few other diseases do. As a caregiver, you will miss the give and take of your relationship with your loved one. Jim developed aphasia early on in the disease. He changed from a man who laughed and joked and shared his deepest thoughts with me to one who seldom spoke a word. He once could play any instruments with strings, but gradually he struggled to play his guitar. Jim had known the lyrics to several hundred songs, but eventually, he would only attempt a few songs and often sang only the chorus over and over. I missed meaningful communication with my husband. Our relationship gradually evolved and each transition increased the loneliness.

Another factor of loneliness is that some friends back away, especially when those friendships involve another couple. Activities are no longer the equal friendships from before and your loved one cannot participate at the same level. Other friends may simply not know what to say or how to react to odd behavior. You will learn to rely on the ones who take the changes in stride and continue to support you in your changing roles.

Spending time with trusted friends or family who make your loved one feel part of the group is a good way to combat loneliness. These special people can lend some normalcy to a world that at many times seems anything but normal.

Simple activities can create awkward situations. Eating out can be a challenge. Once, we went out to eat at a nice restaurant with our friends Rick and Robbie. We all know how cold restaurants can be, and with Jim on blood thinners, he began to shiver uncontrollably. Robbie went to their car and returned with a blanket that she wrapped around Jim. After our meal came, we discovered that the fish Jim ordered had bones in it. Noticing that it looked like Jim didn't remember how to remove the bones, his old fishing buddy, Rick, took a steak knife and filleted the fish leaving him only the boneless portion to eat.

We often socialize with friends based on an activity that we have in common. Whether you play golf, play cards, ride motorcycles, or have backyard barbecues, a loss of skill may make continuing as a couple impossible, or dangerous. Your loved one may also become uneasy in crowds or a different environment causing him distress and anxiety for you. People who are more casual acquaintances, may not realize the activity is no longer appropriate for your loved one. It may be simpler to turn down invitations, increasing the gap between you and your friends.

To keep from being left out of all the fun, you can plan a get-together with a small group where your loved one is more comfortable. Or, you may want to find someone to stay with your loved one so that you can enjoy an outing. You don't want to isolate yourself from people who can support you and offer you companionship.

Widen your circle of friends by joining a club, volunteering, or attending charity events. Being a part of these groups will not only help you find new friends, but it can also keep you busy while making a worthwhile contribution to your community.

I found the best way to battle loneliness was to be comfortable with being alone. After the tough decision to place Jim in a nursing home, I returned to school to earn my bachelor's degree. Working full time and studying for my classes didn't leave much time to feel sorry for myself or to feel lonely. One of the better decisions I made was to join a local business women's group. Our town is small, but our local is the largest Business Women of Missouri club. I've made friends with women throughout Missouri that I would never have known otherwise. I also joined two writers' guilds. I gained a new group of friends where I found encouragement, support, and learned invaluable information to build on my desire to write. Whatever your interests, you can combat loneliness by taking a chance on joining with like-minded people.

Yes, Alzheimer's is a lonely disease, but keeping active is your best defense. Don't be afraid to leave your comfort zone, especially when you are feeling sad and alone. After all, loneliness is an emotional response to isolation, so surround yourself with friends and family who uplift you and fill your need for interaction with others through the giving and receiving of friendship.

Caregiver Emotion #6 – Defensiveness

After the Alzheimer's diagnosis, you probably delved deep to find all the information you could to be the best caregiver possible. You searched reliable sources on the Internet, contacted the Alzheimer's Association for educational opportunities, and attended support group to learn about first-hand experiences. After all your work and dedication to caregiving, cousin Sally breezes in for a ten minute visit and proceeds to list things that you are doing wrong and critiquing your job as a primary caregiver. Is it any wonder you become defensive?

Now, before you push Sally out the door and refuse to take any additional calls from her, pause to consider if anything she said had merit. She may not have presented her "help" in the right tone of voice or in a tactful way, but perhaps if you sift through her suggestions, you might find one useful nugget. Since you are the one with experience, and the one who knows your loved one best, you are responsible for using best practices while caring for your loved one, even if your least favorite cousin Sally suggested it.

When you are a caregiver for a person with Alzheimer's, you learn how your loved one reacts to environmental changes. It may not take much to throw everything out of kilter. A gathering of friends and family may once have been something you looked forward to, but now you know it will only confuse the person you are caring for. Rather than just being defensive if someone criticizes your change in entertainment patterns, take a few minutes to explain that circumstances have changed. You don't want to isolate your loved one, but it will be helpful for friends and family to visit in small groups rather than hosting big events.

One place you do need to be defensive is if anyone tries to take advantage of your loved one. During the early stages, Jim was the telemarketer's best friend. It seemed he always agreed to their suggestions. It wasn't unusual to come home after work and have Jim say. "Someone called about that thing."

"What thing?"

"You know, that we want."

"Who called?"

"I have no idea."

After a few of those conversations, I installed caller ID. I often had to call to cancel TV programs, donations to various charities, tickets to events we couldn't attend, and occasionally say no to people we knew who really should have known not to make agreements with Jim.

Primary caregivers have to be defensive when it comes to protecting the person with dementia, but not let defensiveness keep them from accepting help or valuable information. As with every aspect of caring for a person with Alzheimer's, you need to control emotions, like defensiveness, in order to make the best caregiving decisions.

Caregiver Emotion #7 – Grief

A primary caregiver has a tremendous emotional stake in meeting his or her responsibilities to a loved one. Although taking care of the physical needs of someone who has Alzheimer's is challenging, a survey of caregivers revealed that their biggest challenge was grief.

When you are a caregiver, your grief is anticipatory. Once you've heard the diagnosis and accepted the inevitable outcome, you can't help but grieve about the future. The future looks bleak, and you may want to grab time and make it stand still.

My first reaction after hearing the Alzheimer's diagnosis was, "There is medicine for that, isn't there?" I had paid scant attention to Alzheimer's, but had heard that treatments had been developed. It was a real wake up call to find out the treatment for Alzheimer's only helps with symptoms and does not slow down, much less stop, the disease.

Grief for a caregiver is also ambiguous, without a defined beginning or end. You may not begin to grieve until you've completed tests to rule out treatable conditions. Since Alzheimer's is often diagnosed by ruling out other possibilities, you may go through a time when you think that what your loved one has will get better with time. Some of the theories we heard: depression, low blood sugar, vitamin B deficiency, stroke. It's pretty bad when you latch onto the possibility of a stroke. Yes, strokes are bad, but there is hope that you can recover from a stroke.

After all the tests, and treatments for other possible conditions, Jim continued to lose more skills. So when did the grieving process begin? I'm just not sure. Was it the day he asked me to tune his guitar? Jim was a master musician who played by ear and it always seemed magical to me how he could hear the slightest nuance when something was out of tune. Me, I can't tune a guitar, never could, and never will be able to, and Jim should have known that. Could it have been the day I realized he could no longer read the books he loved? Maybe it was the time he couldn't remember how to work the remote control.

I really don't remember the day when the grieving started, and I can't remember when it stopped. All I know is that it was always there right beside me throughout the years of dementia and loss. It didn't even stop when he died. I know people often say their grieving is done before death happens. Well, it didn't work that way for me. Death was another loss in a series of losses. I wasn't able to shut the grief off magically.

Little things often remind me of the great big hole Jim left behind. After I figured all the grieving was finished, and I'd put it behind me, I noticed it at odd times. There was the day I decided to donate his clothes to charity. Yeah, I know I should have done it sooner. I could have given away his clothes once I realized he wouldn't be wearing anything other than sweatpants, T-shirts, or sweatshirts. No, I waited. I was doing pretty well until I came across his very favorite shirt. I just couldn't part with it. Maybe someday I'll be able to, but it felt like trying to let go of his memory and I wasn't ready.

That's the thing about grief. It's personal and lives inside of us. No one can make another person let go of the grief until it is time. You won't wake up one morning and find that the grief has just gone away. Nope. It leaves when it's good and ready.

The thing about grief is, you learn to live with it until you can live without it. Eventually, you begin to look forward to each new day and to life. You develop a greater appreciation of family and friends. You have learned that time is much too precious to waste, and you refuse to let unbridled grief steal it away. The best way to honor the memory of a person you loved and lost is to live life to the fullest.

Cousins' Reunion

My mom and dad both came from big families and I have a hundred or so cousins. Growing up, I knew my Whittle cousins quite well. We saw each other frequently at Grandma and Grandpa Whittle's house in Stover. The ones close to my age became like additional sisters to me. Younger kids seemed like pests at the time, but I still formed a family bond with them.

I never had the same close attachment with my cousins on my dad's side of the family. My only contact with them was during sporadic family reunions, usually at my Aunt Freida's house. Because of the reunion location, the cousin I saw most consistently on the Capps side of the family was Karen. I was in my early teens when I met my cousins Charlie and Sharyn, but we became pen pals and they both came to my high school graduation.

Time passed and it seemed that I only saw my cousins at funerals, usually with little time to visit and become reacquainted. When Charlie died, my mom and I went to the funeral. Sharyn was heartbroken to lose her only sibling. We exchanged addresses but our written communication was limited to Christmas cards. Jim was in the nursing home in Marshall where Sharyn lived, and we occasionally had lunch together. A few years ago, my Christmas card was returned, and I never received one from her with a new address.

It is easy to lose touch with people and yet with Facebook it is so easy to connect. Last winter, my cousin Karen suggested that I friend my cousin Marge. Soon, we were talking about a cousins' reunion in the summer.

As the time grew closer, we firmed up a date. My brother Tommy offered to host the reunion. He asked me to get hold of my aunt and uncle that lived in Sedalia and their daughter. I told him I could do that.

"How about Sharyn?" I asked.

"Can you call her?"

"I'm sure I can track her down," I said. "I know her married name, and I think she lives at Marshall."

After we hung up, I placed the call to my aunt and uncle. They were excited about a reunion. Then I tried to find Sharyn on Google. I couldn't find her, so I pulled out an area wide phone book, and there she was—listed at Sweet Springs. I'd been spelling her last name wrong. Oh, well, since all I was looking for was a phone number, I called the number in the book. Busy. After several attempts, I thought, *she's probably on dial up Internet*. The next day, I called and a recording said the number had been disconnected.

My phone book was several years old, so I asked a co-worker, Dawn, if she had a newer directory. She said, "I always look on People Find."

"Oh, I couldn't find her on Google, but I was spelling Sharyn's name wrong." I spelled the name, she typed it in, and then turned to me and said, "It says she's deceased."

"What? No one in the family knew that. Maybe it's not her."

Dawn plugged the name in Google and up popped Sharyn's obituary. She had died two years ago.

After I shared the shocking news with my brother, I realized how important this reunion was. I knew Marge had lost three brothers that I never really had a chance to know.

The day of the reunion was a beautiful sunny, warm summer day. As we sat in Tommy's lanai, we took turns talking about what we did, our families, our passions.

"When I was growing up, I thought Dad had about fifteen brothers and sisters," my sister Terri said. My two aunts at the reunion—Rosemary (Runt) and Freida (Dede) both laughed.

"Dad is the one that gave us the nicknames," Rosemary said.

"I thought Robert did," said my cousin Robin. I nodded agreement. Her mother, Shirley (Tot) had always said my dad had given them the nicknames. Aunt Shirley passed away two years ago, and I remembered her saying the same thing many times.

We heard stories of heartbreak, my brother Jimmy and my cousin Mary had both lost daughters. My cousin Karen shared the humorous story of my mom and Aunt Freida's trip to California to visit her sister "Dude." My aunt Freida stepped off the train to make sure they were on the correct train, and the train left with my mom, my mentally handicapped cousin Laney, my aunt's ticket, purse, and luggage. Even without money or proof of identity, my aunt managed to get on the next train and arrived shortly after my mom and Laney. "That's why we take her now," Karen finished.

"Laney is my favorite cousin," my brother Jimmy said. "She's my biggest fan." Laney beamed from ear-to-ear. My aunt takes her to the nursing home when Jimmy, my mom, and friends play music.

After sharing abbreviated stories of our lives, we moved to the yard for pictures and conversation. My mom, Jimmy, and Mitchell played music with others joining in to sing. Family ties brought us together, but it was the beating heart of family helped us bond.

Tommy Capps, Vietnam Veteran
American Hero

Independence Day is a time for Americans to take stock of their freedom and think about the human sacrifice that has given it to us. As far as unpopular wars, the Vietnam War has to be at the top of the list. We were a country divided, and the very people who risked their lives to fight for our country were not given a heroes' welcome when they returned home.

For the first time, war was brought into American homes on the news each day. Even the blood and gore we saw on TV didn't do justice to the reality of being in a jungle with no way to tell friend from foe.

The Wall in Washington, D.C., lists the names of 58,272 people who lost their lives in Vietnam. Others came home injured in body, and countless others came home with a shattered spirit. Vietnam veterans became a stereotype, and Jim would often turn a TV show off in disgust saying, "Another crazed Vietnam veteran is the killer." Hollywood's idea of a Vietnam veteran was of a trained killer, not a young man who was drafted into jungle warfare against an invisible enemy.

When my eighteen-year-old brother Tommy was drafted and sent to Vietnam, we were all scared for what he would be facing, but my mother was terrified. Three months after his tour of duty began, I woke up one night to hear voices and my mother crying, and I knew it had to be about Tommy. I kept thinking, *he can't be dead or I would feel it.* I finally realized he had been wounded and was in the states.

Recently, my sister-in-law nominated Tommy for the American Hero of the Year award. This time, the phone call was good news when my brother found out he was a finalist for Hero of the Year when he didn't even know he had been nominated.

Tommy has shown courage his entire life. After Vietnam he returned to high school and graduated the same year I did. He was a positive influence on the high school kids, and I'm sure several would-be dropouts continued their education. He worked in law enforcement as a deputy, chief of police, and detective. Eventually, he worked for the state of Missouri investigating child abuse cases. He was instrumental in sending 230 child abusers and pedophiles to prison.

In a five-hundred word essay, Teresa only touched on a few of the highlights. Tommy's family and friends could tell hundreds of stories about how he's made his corner of the world better. How he's been the one you could count on to always do the right thing— maybe not exactly what you asked for, but what you needed.

Tommy has been my hero for years, now America has a chance to make him their hero too. Tommy is already a winner in the contest as well as life.

Search for Missing Missouri Woman With Alzheimer's

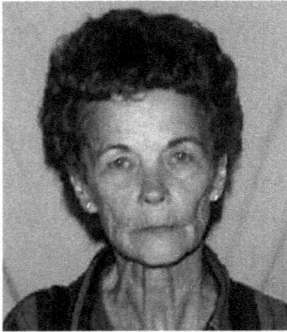

It's every Alzheimer's caregiver's nightmare—a loved one has gone missing and can't be found. On July 13, Hellen Cook tended to yard work while her husband mowed at their home in Warsaw, Missouri. Her husband left for fifteen or twenty minutes to put his mower in the barn, and when he returned, Hellen no longer sat on the porch swing. She had vanished.

Yes, I know that heart-stopping moment firsthand. While we were still seeking a diagnosis for Jim, he accompanied me and several members of our Board of Directors on a business trip to Las Vegas. Everything was going fine until we were at the airport headed home. While I went to get our boarding passes, Jim had to go to the restroom. It was within sight of where I was standing. I finished and then became concerned about why he hadn't returned.

One of the directors went into the restroom to check on him, and discovered he wasn't there. "We'll find him," Francis said, probably with much more confidence than he felt. The directors fanned out and within ten minutes had found Jim.

"He was pretty easy to spot," Don Joe said with a laugh. And he was, wearing a bright red Kansas City T-shirt and a cowboy hat.

That was only the first of many searches. I was by myself when I lost him at the mall. Security helped me find him. Once again, he had gone to the bathroom but went the wrong direction when he came out. I lost him at Silver Dollar City—twice—and one of those times, he had our grandson with him. I learned the hard way that the bathroom had two exits.

All it took was for me to be distracted for a few minutes, and he would be gone. I was folding clothes one time and my sister-in-law called to say Jim was walking down the road in front of their house. One time a neighbor found him several miles from home and close to the highway.

Of all the times he went missing, the scariest one was the night I woke up to discover he wasn't in bed. After I searched the house and realized he was gone, I was frantic. Thankfully, he always stayed on the road and walked the same direction, so I did know where to start looking. I got in the car and found him within a few miles of home. He was fully dressed, complete with dark sunglasses, cowboy hat, and using his cane.

Even the best caregivers can lose track of someone with Alzheimer's. Sixty percent of people with Alzheimer's wander. The Alzheimer's Association has two programs to help with the search efforts. One is MedicAlert + Safe Return. Jim was registered with Safe Return. Although it doesn't keep them from wandering, it does help activate the search immediately. The ID jewelry will alert others that the person is memory impaired and all they have to do is call the toll free number.

A new program, Comfort Zone, uses technology to remotely monitor a person with Alzheimer's. If they leave the pre-set safety zone, family members can be alerted via email, text message, mobile phone, or the internet. I'm excited about this new program and could see how it would be more reliable than counting on neighbors to notice that a person with dementia seems to be lost.

If your loved one is lost, don't search for more than fifteen minutes without calling for help. When you dial 911, tell them a vulnerable adult is missing. Beginning a timely search is crucial to finding your loved one. The Alzheimer's Association shares the statistic that ninety-four percent of people who wander are found within a mile and a half of where they disappeared. The more people who search immediately, the better chance you have of finding your loved one.

Hundreds have joined the search for Hellen Cook, who went missing two weeks ago. Dogs were used early on, but they lost her scent at the highway. That led everyone to believe that she had been picked up by someone in a car. Family, friends, and other volunteers, including the Alzheimer's Association local chapter, conducted a ground search. In a wooded area near a pond they found boots, a scarf, and a hat believed to belong to Hellen.

The search continues for Hellen, and her loved ones are more fearful each day. Please be on the lookout for Hellen, and remember her and her family in your prayers.

Healthy You—Healthy Me

I recently read a featured article in our local paper about people who had joined a program called Healthy U. Candidates are selected for the program and they learn life-changing strategies to help them lose weight and then maintain that weight loss. One woman said her only hesitation was that her "before" weight would be published in the paper.

Now, we all know women when it comes to weight. You can't shave a few pounds off the total when you have a public weigh-in. And you don't have that advantage of weighing in the privacy of your home when you first wake up—before coffee, breakfast, and anything else that seems to make you weigh an extra five pounds. Who ever thought clothing could be so darned heavy!

The Healthy U candidate I admired the most was the lady that hadn't lost any weight at all. In fact, she had gained a few pounds. She had the courage to see the positives in the program. She was healthier and had much more stamina. She looked beyond the tattle-tale scales and saw that she had "gained" health, not weight.

When we think about the things in life that are really important, good health will top that list almost every time. What would it matter if you had accumulated wealth, power, fortune, or fame but did not have good health? We all know people who deal with chronic illness on a daily basis. Then, we have all seen courage and faith improve quality of life for our loved ones who have terminal illnesses.

Anyone that struggles with a health problem that can be controlled through healthy eating and exercise knows that true lifestyle changes require more than good intensions. It requires persistence, diligence, and a serious commitment. I should know. After all, I'm the queen of failed diets and abandoned exercise plans.

I've always been blessed with good health. At least that's how I think of my health since I'm seldom sick. As I've gotten older, I started to find out about all those hidden health markers that undermine my complacency about health. It's not just the number on the scales that keeps creeping upward—it's those pesky lipid panel numbers. Just about the time I think I have one of them licked, a different one sets off the "High" alarm.

Now, I'm working with my new best friend, the dietician. I have a time limit to get the numbers under control or I have to add a new medication to my pill organizer.

I have to admit that it feels good to lose a few pounds, and I don't consider this new approach a diet. It's more of a challenge to make smarter choices. I looked through the list of foods I have to choose from and a funny thing happened. I never saw a single cake, cookie, pie, or donut on there. So, at the dinner meeting last week, dinner was healthy—tilapia—but dessert was cobbler and ice cream. At my request, they served me fresh strawberries and cantaloupe. Since I love both, I enjoyed my dessert.

One of the things I really like about this approach is the dietician asked me what foods I really liked, and she made suggestions for snacks that fell into my favorite foods. When I told her about my weakness for miniature chocolate bars, she said I could have two of them for a snack occasionally.

I'm sure I'll fall off the wagon and have a dessert occasionally, but this is important to me. As I gear up for retirement, good health is at the top of the list. If it takes a little behavior modification on my part, the rewards far outweigh the sacrifices.

Stress and Memory

While browsing through my old health newsletters prior to pitching them, I came across an interesting article on stress and memory. The study involved rats and cats. The rats learned their way through a water maze and were doing quite well until they were placed in cages next to cats. Then, the rats forgot everything they had learned about the maze.

Don't you feel just like a rat trapped in a cage next to your worst enemy some days? If you have the big bad world nipping at your heels, it makes sense that your memory might fail you at the most crucial times.

When you consider the strain of being an Alzheimer's caregiver, it is no wonder that memory is not just a concern for the person with the disease. Each stage of caregiving involves both emotional and physical stressors according to the *Alzheimer's Association's 2013 Alzheimer's Disease Facts and Figures* (p.33). Research shows that caregiver's who are responsible for a person with Alzheimer's or a related dementia report higher stress levels than caregivers of older adults with other diseases.

In the United States, 15.4 million family, or unpaid, caregivers provide $17.5 billion worth of care to their loved ones with dementia. Family caregivers provide an average of nine hours care per day.

Sixty-one percent rated emotional stress as very high and another thirty-nine percent rated the level as somewhat high. When the stress levels are broken down further, fifty-six percent report "a good amount" of strain due to financial issues and another fifty-three percent cite family relationships.

The role of the primary caregiver intensifies as the disease progresses, which creates health issues for the caregiver. Stress suppresses the immune system leaving caregivers vulnerable to physical problems. Caregivers who report the highest levels of stress are those who feel obligated to take on the role of caregiver.

In addition to the stress and strain of being a dementia caregiver, you may have a little niggling thought that perhaps your memory isn't what it should be. You know firsthand what a devastating disease Alzheimer's is, and with your responsibilities, you can't possibly give up or give in to the doubts plaguing you about your own memory problems.

I think the only thing that really kept me from believing I was developing dementia on my own was the knowledge that dementia affects so much more than memory. It chips away at long-term skills, not just those recently learned. Yes, short-term memory is the first symptom, but when you consider the effect stress has on memory, stress is a more likely scenario than dementia.

An important characteristic for a caregiver is optimism. With Alzheimer's, your positive hopes for a cure are dashed, but that doesn't mean you can't do countless acts that will increase the quality of life for your loved one. Continue to do as much as you can together for as long as possible. Those days spent on drives, picnics in the park, walking hand-in-hand on a nice spring day will not only relieve the stress of caregiving, but also will remain forever in your heart.

Perhaps, like me, you have already noticed stress affects your ability to recall information. Before you get too stressed out about your memory, think about rats and cats. The best antidote for stress is relaxation.

Anything you can do to help lower your stress levels will improve your memory. Quiet time is so important and time away, respite, can be a lifesaver for a caregiver. You are not being selfish by needing that time. When you improve your physical or emotional health, you become a better caregiver. Your own health is one of the best gifts you can give your loved one.

Update: Hellen Cook's Family Mourns

Sunday, August 11, Hellen Cook's family received word that human remains were discovered near the search area where her scarf and shoes had been found in July. Pending DNA identification, her family has identified jewelry as belonging to the seventy-two-year-old woman who had Alzheimer's disease. Her husband of fifty years expressed his fear that she had been calling out for him, and he couldn't find her. Please remember this family in your prayers.

Wandering is a serious issue. Sixty percent of people with dementia will wander and if not found within twenty-four hours half of them will suffer serious injury or death.

From the Alzheimer's Association (www.alz.org):

The Alzheimer's Association encourages individuals and families coping with wandering to enroll in MedicAlert + Alzheimer's Association Safe Return®, a nationwide identification program designed to assist in the return of those who wander and become lost.

Families seeking a more technologically advanced and robust program may consider the new Alzheimer's Association Comfort Zone program. Family members can have knowledge of a person's location, while individuals with Alzheimer's can enjoy the emotional security of familiar routines and surroundings.

For more information about Comfort Zone, Medic Alert + Alzheimer's Association Safe Return or additional tips on coping with wandering and other safety issues related to dementia and Alzheimer's disease, visit www.alz.org/safetycenter or call the Association's 24/7 Helpline at 1.800.272.3900.

Those Days Have Come and Gone

Maybe it was because my grandkids went home and the house was too quiet. Maybe it was just the thought of growing older and retiring. Whatever caused it, I had dreams of my brother Donnie, of Jim, and days long gone by. We were all younger in my dreams. As I awakened from a deep sleep the words echoed through my head, "Those days have come and gone."

It's hard to understand the world of dreams. Sometimes they inspire me to write short stories or provide a scene for my novel in progress. This time, the dreams weren't so important, or unusual, it was the truism that stood out from my night's sleep.

The past is a part of me that lingers in my mind just to be awakened in my alternate life—dreamland. Dreams can seem so real at the time. It made me think of Poe's "A Dream Within a Dream." Reality blurs with dreams, and it is possible to cling to the past of a "surf-tormented shore" while we watch the sands of our lives slip through our hands.

Unlike Poe, I choose to not weep and fall into despair over the days that have come and gone. Yes, at times, it is more challenging to put the past aside than others. Keeping busy, working toward goals, feeling a sense of accomplishment are tools to push away the dark sadness of another time gone forever, another place that no longer exists.

Yet, the very busyness that helps keep the past from tormenting, can also cause regret. Sometimes, I have to choose between obligations and inclinations. If I'm not careful, I find myself having regrets that I let work interfere with family time. But if I'm realistic, which I am most of the time, I realize that work has been a beneficial part of my life in more than a financial sense. When Jim was in need of constant care, I needed work as a diversion from the overwhelming job of caregiving.

Being around my grandkids this week reminded me of when my kids were young. Instead of just grabbing something, anything, to eat, I needed to think about meal planning, like when my sons were small. Even going to the State Fair took on a retro atmosphere. It had been years since I stood on the Midway while the kids ran from one carnival ride to another. I'm older, slower, and somewhat wiser now. I wore comfortable shoes and used the umbrella I carried to shade me from the sun.

It was a week that took me back in time, but with changes. Okay, I'll admit that I'm about a thousand times more indulgent with my grandkids than I was with my children. My XM radio station was on the Disney channel all week. My TV was tuned to cartoons and pre-teen shows. I went to the movies, twice. I drove by Kentucky Fried Chicken and ordered above the sound of the "La la la-la" Smurf happy song. The question of the day became, "Is a Smurf's butt blue?"

Just like in my dream, the past week of a house filled with laughter, thumps, and bumps from morning to bedtime have come and gone. It took me by surprise how much I missed it the instant the house took on its usual quiet, peaceful atmosphere.

I decided to go work for a few hours to take my mind off it. I pulled my car out of the garage and the radio began to play "Chloe, You're the One I Want." I'd heard that song a dozen times in the past few days. I shook my head and twisted the dial pausing on Escape, Praise, 80's on 8, and finally rested the dial on 60's on 6. It was obvious that those days had come and gone. I punched the button my granddaughter had set and listened to some here and now music to appreciate the blessing of today and the tomorrows that are mine to enjoy.

Turn Up the Heat

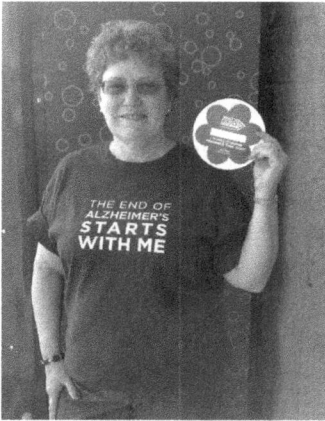

A group of four volunteers sat outside Walmart Saturday morning with forget-me-nots and Walk to End Alzheimer's information. This has been an annual event for the past several years. When Sheila and I first set up, it seemed that no one was going to make eye contact and our "Good morning" greetings often when unanswered. I couldn't help but think that this was going to be a waste of time.

We arrived early—eight thirty—in hopes of beating the heat. We've gone through the entire summer with unusually cool weather, and here we were outside on a day when the thermometer was predicted to zoom into the nineties.

After thirty minutes, flies began to buzz and the sun barreled down on the spot where we had set up our table. "Do we dare move it any closer?" I asked eyeballing the small spot of shade between the soda machine and the trashcan. "We don't want to be so close that the door stays open."

We left our table where it was and moved into the small spot of shade. Then, people began to stop and ask about the Walk and about Alzheimer's. The morning had started getting interesting. They placed donations into our collection jar and we had them write names on the forget-me-nots. Sometimes they wrote a loved one's name. Other times, they wrote their own name. I handed the marker to a little boy and he signed with scribbles.

"How old is he?" I asked.

"He's four. His name is Cash."

I smiled. It never occurred to me that he was too young to write, and of course, he would have a distinctive name. Most kids do now-a-days.

"Sheila, with all the nice weather we've had this summer, why did we pick the hottest day to schedule this?"

"Well, we didn't know it was going to be this hot," she pointed out. I used a forget-me-not for a fan and she used a flyer.

From time to time, we saw people we knew, but most passersby were strangers to us. Most had the story of loss that paves the path of the Alzheimer's journey.

Our donation jar filled up with dollars, fives, tens, and one twenty. The forget-me-not skirt around our table grew in length.

We handed out team packets and donor envelopes. People just walked past and stuffed in dollars. Their voices murmured, "Mom," "grandpa," "husband," "friend..."

One woman wrote a name on a flower and said, "My mom won't go see the doctor, but we're pretty sure she has Alzheimer's."

I handed her a brochure. "Call the number on the bottom. They will help you even though you don't have a diagnosis. Encourage your mom to get a medical workup to find out if she doesn't have

Alzheimer's. Other conditions can cause dementia symptoms and some are reversible."

"Thank you so much!" she said. "I never thought of that."

Then, the highlight of my day—a woman named Betty told us about a new Alzheimer's Support Group. Our group had dwindled, and we stopped having regular meetings. People call me from time to time about support group and I refer them to the chapter and offer to meet with them. Now, a woman stood in front of me telling me that she was going to have the required training to be a support group facilitator. I wrote down the information.

"An Alzheimer's article is coming out in *The Democrat*," I said. "She wants some information for a side-bar and this is so timely."

Shortly after meeting Betty, Wyann brought the forget-me-nots and donations they had collected at the other entrance. Soon, Jessica and Samantha brought over the money they had collected at Big Lots. She also brought the yummy looking cupcakes she had left over.

It felt like Mother Nature had turned up the heat, and although we had rearranged our table to be in the shade, we were sweltering.

"Well, now we need to stay until all the cupcakes are gone," Sheila said.

"I'm game," I replied, "but I'm tired of drinking hot water. I'll go to McDonald's and get us some iced tea."

Two hours later, the iced tea was almost gone, and the last two cupcakes went to a woman who had four kids. "They can share," she said.

As we packed up and folded the table, Sheila said, "You know, it was hot, but it was fun."

"It was! I feel good about it," I said. "I'm so excited about the Walk!" I took my things to my car and headed back to the store to get the items on my shopping list.

As I neared the entrance, a man holding two shopping bags said, "Whew, it's getting hot out here, isn't it?"

"It sure is," I agreed just as I felt a blast of cold air from the open door. The heat is on in Missouri, but that isn't going to stop us from doing what we can about Alzheimer's.

Why I Walk to End Alzheimer's

Jim is the reason I walk in the Walk to End Alzheimer's.

I think I loved him from the first day we met when his Uncle Orvie introduced us outside the Dew Drop Inn in Stover. It was by chance that Jim was in Missouri since he spent a lot of his growing up years in Oregon, Idaho, Utah, California... Jim loved to travel and we often went to Oregon to visit his relatives and childhood places. Later, we went to Estes Park and the Rocky Mountains annually.

Jim was a talented musician who loved to play his Fender guitar and sing country songs. I remember one time I taped him with our gigantic video camera singing "Colorado" while chipmunks and tourists stopped everything to just soak up the sunshine, clear mountain air, and melody. Jim's life was cut short when he developed dementia at forty-nine. He passed away in 2005 after ten years living with a disease that robbed him of his talents, sense of humor, and thoughtful conversation.

Jim lives in my memory and dreams, and I know that he is not forgotten by his family and friends. We need to stop this disease before more families go through the loss and pain of Alzheimer's disease and other dementia. Walks are held across the country. Join a walk near your hometown. Walk for Jim. Walk for your loved ones. Walk for more than five million Americans with this incurable progressive disease.

Walk to End Alzheimer's 2013

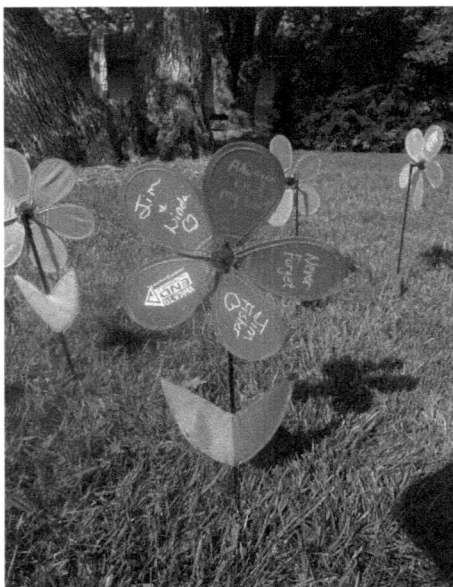

We had a bright sunshiny, warm day for our 2013 Walk to End Alzheimer's at the Missouri State Fairgrounds Saturday morning. I was there bright and early—6:30 a.m.—along with other volunteers and members of the committee. Sheila and I played traffic cops as we directed placement of tables, conferring as to whether that table might work better here or there.

For once, we didn't have to worry about rain, but heat was a concern with temps expected to soar into the upper nineties. At the last minute, while a volunteer was on his way to get more ice, we asked him to buy more water too. Walkers began to arrive and organized chaos took over as teams began to group together.

My sister-in-law, Ginger, started the cake walk, Kim and Bobby Brown manned the raffle table (which may have helped them rest up for awhile after bringing a trailer load of tables and chairs), Sheila grabbed the microphone and began to make announcements, registration tables were manned, and on my table, I arranged books to sign and give to walkers.

As I signed, I chatted with friends and family who came up to get a copy of *Focus on the Positive*. I also met new friends who came to the walk for the first time this year. As I was signing, a woman walked up wearing a shirt that said "Hellen's Heroes." I knew she was on the team honoring Hellen Cook, the woman with dementia whose body was found after nearly a month long search. Hellen was Darolyn's mother, and she introduced me to her brother Mike. My heart went out to this family who lived through a caregiver's worse nightmare. They have taken this tragedy and turned it into a positive by proposing "Hellen's Law" to tighten up the procedure to report an endangered missing person. I had my picture taken with members of Hellen's Heroes and felt an instant connection with Darolyn.

Later as I was signing books, Linda Newkirk, executive director of the Greater Missouri Chapter, was explaining the significance of the pinwheel flowers and Jim's Team held our purple flowers high to show that we had lost a loved one. Others held up orange, blue, and yellow flowers as their colors were explained. Shortly after, Sheila came to my table and told me I needed to go up to the front where Linda was speaking.

She finally dragged me away. When I got there, Linda was talking about Hellen Cook's family and their advocacy. Then, Linda Newkirk announced that the chapter is placing a brick in their Garden of Hope in recognition of my volunteer work and advocacy. I felt so honored! Even after all these years, I still feel the Chapter did more for me than I can ever do for them. They were my lifeline for ten years while Jim and I traveled the Alzheimer's journey.

Sheila, my granddaughter, and I dropped our pinwheels into a bucket and took the lead as four hundred walkers began the walk. Instead of finishing the walk, we stopped and cheered others on as they came down the shaded walkway. We headed back to the Highway Gardens. Volunteers were planting the pinwheel flowers in the Promise Garden. The breeze turned the pinwheels and tears pricked my eyes to see the expressions of love.

I walked through the Promise Garden snapping photos and found the flower I had decorated for Jim. The breeze continued to turn the pinwheels nearby, but it was as if Jim's flower stopped to pose for the photo. I snapped the photo, and the pinwheel resumed spinning.

Wandering and Silver Alert Legislation

Jim wandered off many times after he developed Alzheimer's. The first thing I learned as a caregiver was immediate action was necessary to find him. I couldn't count the number of times he disappeared. It only took a moment of inattention, or the misconception that someone else had eyes on him. Whether he disappeared mid-morning at a mall in Columbia, early afternoon at Silver Dollar City, late afternoon at the airport in Las Vegas, or from our home in the middle of the night, a search began immediately.

Unfortunately, wandering is a common problem for people with Alzheimer's. Sixty percent of people with dementia will wander causing anxiety for the caregiver and creating a life-threatening situation for the wanderer. Beginning the search immediately is key to finding your loved one safely. Statistics are on your side since ninety-four percent of the time they will be found within one and a half miles of where they disappeared.

You can take a few steps to help find your loved one. Alert neighbors of the situation and ask them to call you if they see your loved one walking alone. When searching, look in the direction of your loved one's dominant hand—that is the direction they will usually go. Use MedicAlert + Alzheimer's Association Safe Return or Comfort Zone (an electronic device). If you don't immediately locate your loved one, call 911 and report them missing.

To ensure that when you call 911, the appropriate steps are taken to activate an immediate search, legislation should be in place. Legislation geared toward a Silver Alert should encompass all persons with dementia regardless of age. Jim had early onset dementia and would have been too young for the Silver Alert in states that identify only persons sixty-five or older with dementia. Missouri has an "Endangered Person Advisory" which could include anyone who may be in danger because of age, health, mental or physical disability, environment, or weather conditions.

If you have a loved one with dementia, it is important to know the laws in your state and work toward legislation to make sure anyone with Alzheimer's is included regardless of age. The law should also have provisions to activate the system based on a caregiver statement since many people wander before they have a formal diagnosis.

An important part of legislation is training for all emergency personnel. Proper training can make all the difference in finding a person with Alzheimer's quickly using search techniques specifically tailored to persons with dementia. The immediate emphasis should be on a search of the local area. Quick and educated response is key to survival.

Silver Alerts are state programs designed specifically for vulnerable adults who have wandered. The search for adults is different from those used for AMBER alerts. AMBER alerts use statewide alerts, which are not typically needed when searching for an adult wanderer. Also, since most wandering adults, like Jim, wander repeatedly, alerting everyone statewide each time an adult wanders could cause the public to become desensitized. This could do more harm than good by reducing the statewide response in cases where it is needed.

The goal is to find wanderers within twenty-four hours and reunite them with their families. The longer the person with dementia is gone, the chances of finding them unharmed are correspondingly diminished.

More than 125,000 search and rescue teams are activated each year to search for missing persons with dementia. This does not include the countless times that family members search for and find their loved ones. Kimberly Kelly with Project Far From Home estimates that as many as three million people with dementia wander away from home each year.

We were fortunate and Jim was always found quickly by either family, friends, neighbors, and during the mall disappearance, security guards. I was young enough to go searching for Jim, but not every vulnerable adult has a caregiver who can look for them. A system needs to be put in place, nationwide, that will activate an immediate search for vulnerable adults with a goal to provide safe return to their homes.

NIH & NIA Fulfill $45 Million Pledge

Earlier this week, Dr. Francis Collins, director of the National Institutes of Health (NIH) fulfilled his promise to Alzheimer's advocates to designate $40 million from his 2013 budget for Alzheimer's research. I was one of more than 700 advocates at the Alzheimer's Association Advocacy Forum, where Dr. Collins announced he was taking this unique step to show the NIH's commitment to finding a cure for a disease that has baffled scientists for decades.

During his keynote address on April 23 at the forum, Dr. Collins said, "I so wish it could be more, but I hope you hear in this kind of a commitment the way in which we at NIH see this as an opportunity and responsibility. We also hope that moving forward we can put medical research back on the stable track that is needed in order to support the research and the researchers."

The story in last week's *New York Times* and *USA Today* both report that an additional $5 million has been designated by the National Institute on Aging (NIA) to provide support for innovative clinical trials.

Among the trials being supported through these additional funds is the Dominantly Inherited Alzheimer's Network Trials Unit (DIAN-TU) trial at Washington University, St. Louis. Dr. Randy Bateman is the team leader. I met Dr. Bateman several years ago when he accompanied Missouri advocates on our visits with our legislators at the Alzheimer's Forum in Washington, D.C. Hearing firsthand the possibilities of research to find therapies or a cure for early onset Alzheimer's is encouraging in a way that reading about it cannot touch. Dr. Bateman was passionate about his work, confident, and optimistic that a cure can be found for the hereditary form of Alzheimer's that can strike during early adulthood.

The APOE4 trials being conducted by Drs. Eric Reiman and Pierre Tariot at the Banner Alzheimer's Institute in Phoenix will be fully funded in 2013. Several other trials are being funded to move them forward. An Allopregnaolone Regenerative Thera-peutic study at the University of Southern California will evaluate the safety and tolerance of a natural brain steroid to treat Alzheimer's disease. Other studies will analyze data collected from volunteers to identify promising therapies, test existing drugs currently used for other conditions for effective treatment of Alzheimer's, and treatment based on targeting the immune system.

In a letter I received as an Alzheimer's Ambassador, Alzheimer's CEO Harry Johns said that the fulfillment of NIH's pledge is historic. "In addition to fueling much needed research toward treatment, prevention, and ultimately a cure, it shows the growing recognition that our cause is receiving at the nation's highest levels." Johns praises hundreds of Ambassadors and hundreds of thousands of advocates for making the case in Washington, D.C., and in communities nationwide. In the Alzheimer's Association news release, Johns said, "These studies are examples of the quality research in the pipeline that needs further funding in order to prevent and effectively treat Alzheimer's disease by 2025 as outlined in the National Alzheimer's Plan."

Kudos to NIH and NIA for taking this first step toward prioritizing research for Alzheimer's. Now, we need to keep pressing our legislators to take a proactive approach to finding a cure for this disease.

Alzheimer's is an equal opportunity disease. It affects people without regard to race, religion, financial status, political party, intelligence, education, or any other classification you can think of. No human is immune to Alzheimer's. It could happen to you or to someone you love if it hasn't already.

It's not a question of whether we can afford the research for Alzheimer's, the real question is—can we afford not to fund research? Does it make sense to spend only $484 million on research that costs this country more than $140 billion annually in Medicare and Medicaid? Alzheimer's is the sixth leading cause of death in the United States, yet the funding is minuscule when compared to research spent on other diseases which received billions annually to fund research.

Some of us have spent years advocating for Alzheimer's research dollars. It can be frustrating when funding is stagnant, or worse yet, the years funding was cut. By hanging tough, advocates have fought for treatment equity for those living with Alzheimer's and other dementias.

This is not the time to rest on our laurels; it is the time to step up our advocacy while the focus is on research. The ultimate goal is a world without Alzheimer's, and it can be done.

That's History

When a day is done, whether good or bad, it immediately becomes history. One of the things about history is that you can't go back and change it; nor can you go back and relive it.

As far as history goes, we all learn important dates in school. In fact we learn more dates than we can ever remember. Sometimes our teachers help us devise tricks to remember and with a little rhyme, we might always remember a date. "In fourteen hundred ninety-two, Columbus sailed the ocean blue." How could I ever forget that date?

That's history class. I always enjoyed history, outside of the date thingy. History is stories...important stories...about events that shape us now, although most school kids think history is boring. The reason it is boring to kids is because the rich stories of the past are reduced to facts and dates, and some of those are presented in a biased and controversial manner. It is interesting to hear that sometimes important events are skipped in the history that children are taught today.

Each of us has a personal history with dates that stick in our minds to be re-examined annually. We have birth dates, death dates, anniversaries, graduations, and a myriad of other events not only to mark time, but also to remember. Is it any wonder that with all these dates stuck in our heads, buried deep inside our brains, that we sometimes forget an appointment or a loved one's birthday?

Today's date takes me back to a day twenty-three years ago when I saw my dad leave this world. It was on the anniversary of his own dad's death. I called my mom tonight and we talked about a lot of things before she brought up the date. I knew it was on our minds from the first "hello."

Our brains are so complex that we can't even comprehend all that goes on between our ears. I can't visualize how many a billion is whether I'm talking about dollars or nerve cells in my brain. Understanding my brain would be a lot like understanding how I can write words on a keyboard and have this computer take those words and allow me to put them on the Internet where anyone can read them. Perhaps, as perplexing is to comprehend how anyone can totally understand how that process actually works.

Historical facts we learned, and our own personal history, is stored in our brains. We have much more stored in our brains than we can ever retrieve. If you are like me, you know it's there, but can't retrieve it at the moment you want it. For instance, if you are playing a game of Trivial Pursuit and you know the answer, but can't remember what it is until immediately after the time is up. Worse yet, you need to know an important piece of information and instead of remembering it at the crucial time, you remember it in the middle of the night.

Memory and history are two parts of the same thing. When two people share a history, and Alzheimer's subtracts that connection, it is a loss for both. Our page in history is our life story, and we want that story to be action packed, suspenseful, and with a glorious ending. With personal history, the dates are not nearly as important as the stories. The only test in life, is a test of self.

Take a Whiff of Jif to Test for Alzheimer's

After hearing about the expensive tests for Alzheimer's, researchers came up with a cheap screening test. The amazing thing about this test is you may already have the necessary item in your pantry— a jar of peanut butter.

Known as the brief olfactory test, taking a whiff of Jif, or any peanut butter for that matter, can help a researcher determine if you have Alzheimer's. Anyway, that was the news out of the University of Florida.

It's commonly known that Alzheimer's affects the sense of smell. Other studies have been done on the olfactory system and Alzheimer's disease. This is not the first! According to a 1989 study published in the *International Journal of Neuroscience*, researchers believed that the changes occurring in Alzheimer's starts in the cortical region of the brain, the region that controls our sense of smell. In 2010, the Alzheimer's Association and the National Institutes of health funded a study that showed that Alzheimer's mice could not distinguish odors as well as other mice. At that time, the researchers noted that an olfactory test could be an inexpensive way to diagnose Alzheimer's.

Fast forward to 2013 and we have the peanut butter whiff test. Jennifer Stamps, a graduate student at the University of Florida's McKnight Brain Institute, conducted the test on ninety people. Some of the people had Alzheimer's or other types of dementia and others had mild cognitive impairment (MCI). Although researchers did not know which people had which problem when they conducted the tests, they were surprised to find that the Alzheimer's patients reacted to the sniff test differently than the other groups.

Here's how the test was conducted: A tablespoon of peanut butter was put on a metric ruler and one nostril was checked at a time. Eighteen of the study group had early-stage Alzheimer's, and they all had one thing in common—trouble smelling the peanut butter out of their left nostril. The group with other types of dementia did not have this problem. The results of the twenty-four people with MCI were mixed—ten had trouble with the left nostril but fourteen didn't. Is this an indication that the ten will go on to develop Alzheimer's disease? Time will tell.

Other researchers urge caution due to the small number of cases included in this study. Others note that head trauma, sinus problems, or congestion can affect the results of an olfactory test. In fact, my friend Donna can't smell anything after an accident that happened when she was a teenager.

So, are you tempted to grab a jar of peanut butter and sniff away? Being the curious person I am and having seen the devastating effects of dementia, I did exactly that. Right nostril, a-okay! One down, one to go. Second nostril—nothing, *nada*, zip, zero. Oh, I did not like this test. Not one little bit.

Time to analyze the test results. Let's see. Left nostril. Come to think of it, I just came off a ten day supply of antibiotics for a left ear infection. So I'm sure that could have affected my sense of smell in my left nostril. Anyway, that's my story and I'm sticking to it. The peanut butter test should come with a disclaimer: Don't try this at home.

Sleep to Ward Off Alzheimer's

We've all heard how important sleep is to our health. Now, a new study published in *JAMA Neurology* indicates that a lack of sleep might increase our chances of developing Alzheimer's. Or, is it the other way around? Does Alzheimer's lead to a lack of sleep?

Jim always considered sleep "a waste of time." He was an early riser his entire life. I, on the other hand, could barely function without eight hours sleep.

Once Jim developed dementia, he seemed to require only about four hours a night. Over time, I too shortened my sleeping hours. Between Jim and being at work by seven o'clock, I just flat didn't have time to sleep much. My eight hours dwindled to six or less. I knew it wasn't good for my health, but chronic lack of sleep became the norm.

A common New Year's resolution for me was to get more sleep. I've struggled with health problems that may have gone away completely with enough shut-eye. One of the side effects of sleep deprivation is weight gain. In some ways that seems counter-intuitive. At one time I figured the longer I was awake, the more calories I would burn and that would make it easier to lose weight. Wrong. It takes sleep to regulate the hormones that tell us when we are hungry. When ghrelin and leptin are not balanced, we think we are hungry which leads to overeating.

Instead of sleep being a waste of time, we are at our most productive while we are catching our ZZZ's. When we move into the deepest stage of sleep, our bodies move into restorative overdrive. While we sleep, we are recharging our energy levels. Our muscles relax and our blood pressure drops. Hormones essential for tissue growth and repair are released. During sleep, we consolidate everything we've learned which improves our memory.

On the flip side of the sleep coin, lack of sleep quality or quantity may lead to serious health disorders—heart disease, stroke, diabetes—to name a few. A couple of other distressing side effects are depression and premature aging.

Researchers have known for years that people who don't get enough sleep are forgetful. This new study takes that concern to an entirely different level. Researchers at Johns Hopkins Bloomberg School of Public Health in Baltimore used scans to measure the buildup of beta-amyloid plaques, one of the hallmarks of Alzheimer's disease. Even healthy people can have some plaques in their brains, but they do not have as many as those with Alzheimer's. The people who did not get enough sleep had more buildup of plaques in their brains than those who reported that they slept well at night.

Why would sleep have anything to do with beta-amyloid plaques? It seems that while we sleep our brain is in self-cleaning mode. During sleep our brain cells shrink which allows cerebrospinal fluid to wash away the toxins in our brain.

Of course, this all comes with a disclaimer that sleep might not stop Alzheimer's, but anything that will reduce the formation of cell-choking plaques can be seen as therapeutic. In addition to sleep itself, the researchers believe that drugs should be explored to force the cleansing process that can occur naturally during deep sleep. This study just reinforces the need to explore different avenues of treatment for Alzheimer's.

Could our way of life contribute to an unprecedented increase of Alzheimer's disease, cancer, and heart disease? Research shows that healthy eating, exercise, and a good night's sleep work together to prevent a myriad of diseases.

As if daytime isn't enough time to ruin our health, we use evenings to cram in TV, Facebook, volunteer work, meetings, social activities, or heaven forbid we take work home. So much to do, so little time. Then when we fall into bed, our brains are still going full tilt to remind us of what we still have to do, or what we've forgotten to do. Sweet dreams are a long time coming just to be interrupted by the alarm clock letting us know it's time to get up and do it all over again.

Maybe it's time to take a deep breath, spend some quality time relaxing and catch some extra ZZZ's. Sweet dreams may be the answer to some of life's most perplexing health issues.

An Autumn Weekend

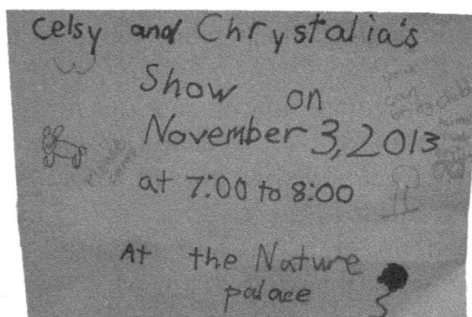

Celsy and Chrystalia's
Show on
November 3, 2013
at 7:00 to 8:00

At the Nature
palace

You always know it is autumn at my house when the ground is littered with walnuts. Even with a handy-dandy walnut picker-upper, they seem to carpet the yard and overflow onto the walkway. Flying leaves and colorful trees leave no doubt as to the season. I left up Halloween decorations while I readied my house for company.

My sister-in-law Sissy and brother-in-law Jim had sold out and were headed to Oregon to live near their children. My nieces, Brenda and Sherry, have spent the past weeks helping, and they were all flying back together. The plan was for them to spend the night, and I would take them to the airport hotel Sunday.

Saturday, they arrived from two different places. Not sure how many were going to be here, I cooked a scary big pot of chili and had deli meats for sandwiches. As people began to arrive, I made pot after pot of coffee. Soon my house was wall-to-wall people. Just like the old days.

The house filled with laughter as we visited. "You know who would have really loved this?" I asked as family gathered in the kitchen. "Jim. He loved spending time with family. Sometimes he would come home and say, 'Oh, by the way, we're having a jam session—and I invited everyone to dinner.' Of course, he'd have no idea just how many were coming."

My niece, Sherry, had her video camera going, just like Jim used to. It reminded me of the two of them talking about their multitude of family tapes. "We'll have the history, Uncle Jimmy. Everyone else will forget, but we can watch our videos and remember." She was correct. So many slices of life would be forgotten without video.

Sherry and I walked out into the yard to reminisce. "We want to reminisce too," chimed in my grand-daughter and great-niece.

"You're not old enough to reminisce," I said.

"I'm half of sixteen," my great-niece said.

The two girls seemed to be joined at the hip. They entertained with dance routines and songs, advertised with posters announcing various show times. They stood on the porch steps, facing the flag, hand over hearts and sang the *National Anthem.* My six-year-old grandson stood at attention and saluted the flag. The scene was amazing and touching, especially considering the flag they used was my autumn "Welcome" flag, with pumpkins on it. In their eyes, it was as valid as the stars and stripes as they sang the song without missing a word.

Sissy and I sat at the table watching the commotion going on outside with four-wheelers, interactions between cousins, older and younger.

"You can sit right here and be entertained," she said.

"It's like watching a reality show, isn't it?" I agreed.

Saturday evening, Sherry and Brenda went to a Halloween party with my son, Rob, and daughter-in-law, Stacey. They came in laughing and joking at midnight. One of the highlights was Brenda winning the costume contest, without a costume. Of course, it helped that Rob was the judge. He said she was dressed exactly like his cousin Brenda from Oregon.

Sunday morning the time change helped us all get up earlier than we thought possible. After coffee, we fixed a big breakfast—biscuits, gravy, sausage, eggs—and then Rob and Stacey tackled how to fit all the Oregon bound family's luggage into the trunk of my car. Amazingly enough, it all fit except a small overnight case.

Early afternoon, we loaded into the car for the drive to the Airport Hilton. We stopped by North Kansas City Hospital so Sissy could visit her sister who had been admitted a few days earlier. Then I took them to the hotel.

Sherry checked them in and Sissy sat in one of the big comfy couches in the lobby. Jim and Brenda were loading luggage onto a cart. When they opened the trunk, I was impressed by the neat arrangement of luggage. There was not an inch of wasted space!

I hugged everyone, determined to keep it light and happy. "I'll be seeing you," I said.

I jumped in my car, drove across the parking lot, and stopped to have OnStar plug in the directions home. As I sat there, I thought of Scotts Mills, Silver Falls, Crooked Finger, the scent of pine on a breezy mountain. Thought of Jim, how he loved Oregon, and visiting his childhood places. But I didn't cry. I just smiled and whispered a prayer for happy trails until we meet again.

November is Alzheimer's Awareness Month

In 1983, President Ronald Reagan declared November Alzheimer's Awareness Month. This year as we mark the 30th anniversary of this event, we have seen both hope and despair on the road to finding effective treatment for a disease that affects over five million Americans.

When President Reagan launched the national campaign to bring an end to a debilitating, fatal disease, he most likely never imagined that he would personally become a victim of Alzheimer's. I know that Jim and I never suspected that this disease would cast its ugly net over our lives.

To be aware of Alzheimer's, you need to take more than a casual glance at the disease. It is not a joke about forgetfulness that afflicts the elderly creating humorous moments of cute memory lapses. Memory is only part of the disease and often the first symptom that others notice.

Alzheimer's is a brain disease. Beta amyloid plaques build up between nerve cells creating sticky clumps that damage the brain's cells ability to communicate with each other. As if this wasn't enough problems, tau tangles interfere with the movement of nutrients from food molecules and other key materials in the brain. Without these essential nutrients, brain cells die.

All this brain chaos follows a predictable pattern in a brain diseased with Alzheimer's. This progression can take up to twenty years!

At first, the disease doesn't seem too bad. During the early stages the person with dementia has memory problems and issues with thinking and planning. When Jim was in the early stages, many people could not see the differences in him that I could. These changes were subtle.

One weekend we went to Manhattan, Kansas, to visit my son. We were going to drive downtown to get a pizza. As we drove down the street, I spotted Pizza Hut. "Turn left," I told Jim.

"Which way?" he asked. That's when I realized that he couldn't tell left from right—at least not when it was spoken. I learned to point to the right or left.

Also, in the early stages, Jim developed aphasia. He was a voracious reader, but began to buy multiple copies of the same book because he couldn't follow the story line and didn't remember reading it a few weeks earlier.

Eventually, Jim progressed to a moderate or middle stage of the disease where his symptoms became more pronounced. His appearance changed a little as he moved into what I considered to be a more eccentric stage. He wore his denim jacket year round and decorated it with pins and the Veterans Week name tag from Branson. He wore dark sunglasses and used a cane. He just looked different and began to act more childlike. Jim was docile and agreeable—neither of which were normal traits for him. He became more silent, his speech hesitant. Jim had been a talented musician and could play any instrument with strings, and knew hundreds of songs. Eventually, he could barely play and could remember only a few songs and often repeated the same line many times.

Reality set in for me during the middle stage. Caregiving became a challenge, and I worried about Jim's safety. He began to wander, and managed to get away from me, other family and hired caregivers. We were fortunate and found him each time, but only after heart-stopping moments.

In severe dementia, most of the brain is seriously damaged and begins to shrink. Eventually, we placed Jim in long-term care. At first, he paced constantly, and seemed unaware of most people around him. He stopped talking except for a few words. He had to have assistance with the most basic functions of life. Over time, he began to lose his balance and had to use a Merry Walker, and later a wheelchair, in order to remain mobile. He went through "failures to thrive" when he became gaunt and hollow-eyed.

Jim had dementia for ten years and from the beginning to the end, we did what we could to keep him physically healthy and happy. Some days, it felt like a losing battle, but it was always worth it.

So, during this Alzheimer's Awareness month, I hope that awareness is as close as you get to the disease. I don't believe anyone who hasn't seen Alzheimer's in a loved one can truly understand the all-consuming nature of the disease. I know that I never had a clue about the reality of a disease that erodes lives and steals a loved one away one memory, one skill at a time. It is because of Jim that I understand the need to find effective treatment and a cure for this incurable life-stealing disease.

Congress passed on a unanimous basis the National Alzheimer's Project Act, which created the first National Alzheimer's Plan. The plan is a strategy to fight Alzheimer's and it is crucial that the proposed additional $100 million funding is included in fiscal year 2014 through the appropriations process.

Missouri Senator Roy Blunt is one of twenty-nine members of Congress appointed to a bipartisan budget committee to report budgets by December 13. I urge my fellow Missourians to ask Senator Blunt to remember Alzheimer's and support the National Plan to Address Alzheimer's Disease.

Time Travel

My six-year-old grandson seriously asked me one morning, "Grandma Linda, have you ever time-traveled?"

I don't believe anyone had ever asked me that question before, but it really got me to thinking about time travel. I remember the first time I read H. G. Wells' *The Time Machine* and saw the original movie. The Time Traveler observes that time travel is a fourth dimension and "only another way of looking at Time."

Then, of course, time travel was common on *Star Trek*. I remember one episode when Captain Kirk and the crew from the *Enterprise* went back in time to find themselves in a gunfight against the Earp brothers at the O.K. Corral. They survived when Mr. Spock realized that the time travel was an illusion in their minds.

We travel to the past in our dreams and in sudden flashes of remembrance. Travel to the future can be through daydreams, plans, goals, or intuition. Some claim to see the future in a crystal ball, but I've never had that advantage. Jim's grandma used to see the future in coffee grounds...guess that's a version of reading tea leaves. That her coffee had grounds in the bottom is an indication of how strong it was. I was always afraid to have her read my coffee grounds because she once told a neighbor that her daughter would "come home in a box." And she did after a car wreck.

Anniversaries are a time that make people time travel. Whether it is a personal anniversary or historical anniversary, dates can trigger realistic memory travel. With the fiftieth anniversary of President Kennedy's assassination, I've about overloaded on specials about the shooting in Dallas and the mysteries that linger. Today as a nation, many will collectively time travel to November 22, 1963. We will think about where we were and what we were doing when we heard about the assassination. I heard the news in the hallway at school. We sat on the floor listening to the radio as the tragedy unfolded. I was telling my granddaughter a few weeks ago that we were out of school and at home watching TV when Jack Ruby shot Lee Harvey Oswald.

Before dementia, Jim was a much more effective time traveler than I will ever be. He remembered people, places, and dates from his childhood with more clarity than I could remember the previous week.

One of the cruelties of dementia is how it erases memories. In the earlier stages, long-term memory isn't affected as much as short-term memory, and it seems the person with dementia has effectively time traveled and, in fact, seems to be living in a different time. Once an elderly lady who was in the nursing home with Jim told me that she had to get home because her dad would be really mad that she was out after dark.

Alzheimer's is like entering a time machine that zooms into the past, wiping out the present and future. Eventually, plaques and tangles jam up the moving parts and the fabulous time machine malfunctions leaving the traveler stranded.

So, the answer is "yes." I do time travel. I don't need a machine with whirling dials that I have to enter to travel back and forth in time. Any little nanosecond will do. All I have to do is rev up the fabulous time machine located between my ears to retrieve another place and time. As far as the future, those travels are flashes of "coming attractions" found in the realm of imagination. Yes, I still look forward to the future and would rather travel forward than backward any day.

The mind is the real time machine, and it really *is* just another way of looking at time.

Thirty Days of Thankfulness
Not Your Usual List

November is a time for self-examination and giving thought to our many blessings and giving thanks where thanks are due. Many of my Facebook friends have been posting one thing they are thankful for each day this month.

I've never participated in this delightful idea, but felt compelled to complete my monthly list in one fell swoop. I made the list and entered it into One Note on a sleepless night. After reviewing the list, I realized that I don't remember seeing any of these items on their lists. I always suspected my thought processes might not be the same as the average person, but until now, I've kept some of the weirdness under wraps.

I am thankful for...

1. **Mice.** It's easy to think of mice as pesky rodents with no purpose in life other than leaving droppings behind furniture and chewing up important papers. But mice are extremely important when it comes to medical research in general and Alzheimer's research in particular.

2. **Sleepless nights.** On sleepless nights, my brain goes into creative overdrive. My best ideas come to me in the middle of the night.

3. **Wishes that didn't come true.** Throughout my lifetime, I've made a lot of goofy wishes, and I'm so thankful that they didn't come true. I don't think the life of a fairy princess, a rock star,

superhero, or being married to Paul McCartney is what God had in mind for me.

4. **People who hurt my feelings when I was young.** Yep, all those cruel kids made me into a rhino-hide adult. It is almost impossible to hurt my feelings, because frankly I don't give a poop about what insensitive, rude people say to me.

5. **Failure.** I've learned more from my failures than I ever learned from my successes. Let's face it, when I make really bad mistakes, I try hard to not do it again.

6. **Not being beautiful.** Being beautiful is a burden I wouldn't want to carry. Besides, I had to work a lot harder on my personality.

7. **Hard times.** There have been times in my life when it was a challenge to figure out how to pay the bills, feed the kids, and not have too much month left at the end of the money. Because of hard times, I've never had that fear of being poor that some people have. Been there, survived, and know that happiness isn't based on the size of my bank account.

8. **Hard work.** Without years of hard work, I wouldn't have done as well in my job as I did and wouldn't be looking forward to retirement.

9. **Having my heart broken.** If a few boys hadn't broken my heart when I was younger, my life would have turned out differently. I'm happy with the way it turned out, so thank you for breaking my heart and forcing me to move on.

10. **Rainy, gloomy days.** When the rain falls and the sun is elusive, it is a perfect time to sleep in and laze around reading a book.

11. **Boredom.** My life is so hectic that if I find time to be bored, I can relax...or think of something totally fun to do.

12. **Hunger.** When I'm hungry, I know I haven't overeaten.

13. **Paying bills.** When I pay bills, it means I have another month of electricity, internet, phone service, and a zero balance on my credit cards.

14. **Not winning the lottery.** I've always known that winning the lottery would screw up my life, and I like it the way it is.

15. **Flies and spiders.** When I'm in a murderous rage, I can squash a spider or swat a fly and not suffer an ounce of guilt.

16. **Clear packing tape and plastic wrap**. The way these two stick to themselves and trying to figure out how to get a roll started teaches me patience.

17. **Old age.** Without old age, I'd have to pay to get into ballgames and wouldn't get senior discounts.

18. **People who don't like me.** They teach me to stand up for myself.

19. **People who take advantage of me.** They keep me on my toes and help me say "no."

20. **Running late.** It's amazing how much time I'd waste waiting if I got to everything early. Besides, I've avoided traffic tickets and dangerous driving when I decided it was better late than never.

21. **Anger.** If an injustice makes me angry, it means I am passionate enough to care.

22. **Fear.** I might not be alive today if I didn't have sense enough to be afraid from time to time.

23. **Ignorance.** Since I clearly don't know everything, ignorance means I always have something to learn.

24. **Grumpy old men.** Without them, grumpy old women wouldn't have anyone to argue with.

25. **Lousy TV shows.** When a lousy show is on TV, it is much easier for me to turn it off and do something productive.

26. **Bratty kids**. I'm so thankful that none of those bratty kids belong to me.

27. **Runny nose.** Without a runny nose, I'm sure my head would explode from the inside out when I have a head cold and infected sinuses.

28. **Thunderstorms and lightning.** We need the rain to replenish the earth and the lightning keeps me honest since I don't want to be struck down for telling a lie.

29. **Bad lab results.** Without bad lab results, I wouldn't have incentive to work toward being healthier. I would have continued the same bad dietary habits with the same results.

30. **Uncertainty.** I don't know everything that is going to happen in my future! Uncertainty keeps me optimistic that the best is going to happen and not the worst.

One of the great things about making a list like this is that it made me realize the thing I am most grateful for is living the life I want and wanting the life I live. I am happy to be me, and I don't envy anybody else's life or want to be somebody I'm not.

Midnight Explosion in Missouri

It exploded like a bomb, shook like an earthquake, sounded like a tornado, looked like a wildfire, felt like the end of the world.

I was having trouble sleeping so I was lying in bed reading a book. I heard an explosion and my windows rattled. If it had stopped there, I would have been fine. Instead, the house shook and shook.

I jumped up out of bed and ran through the house while I tried to figure out what was going on. The way the house was shaking, I thought maybe it was an earthquake. A loud roar sounded more like a tornado, but I had come home at 9:00 p.m. and knew the sky was clear. I had stopped for a moment on the walkway to breathe in the fresh night air and look at the stars.

What could it be? The noise sounded like the entire fleet of Stealth bombers from Whitman circling my house. Had it been a bomb? Had a plane crashed? My heart pounded as I tried to figure out what was going on. The house continued to shake and the rumble was not fading.

I called my son and asked him if he knew what was happening. While I was on the phone with him, I looked out my French doors and the entire sky was lit on the west side of my house. Could a meteor have hit close by? It felt like the end of the world.

"Why don't you just come over here?" Eric asked. He could see the fireball, but it was farther away.

I ran outside, carrying my phone, and I could see flames leaping toward the sky. The sound was even louder. My brother-in-law was in the yard, and like me, he had no idea what we were seeing.

"I'm getting out of here," I said to my brother-in-law. I didn't know what it was, just that it was close, and a roaring, rumbling fire was consuming the night. I jumped in my car and headed away from the explosion. I met car after car rushing toward it. I didn't understand their thinking since no one knew what it was and whether it would explode again. I just knew that distance seemed safer to me.

Eric called back and told me it was a pipeline explosion. Of all the scenarios that had raced through my head, I never once thought of a pipeline explosion. I drove on since I didn't feel confident that it was going to stop with one big blast.

I watched from a distance and for the first time thought to snap a picture on my cell phone. The people rushing toward the explosion, or those with good cameras, captured the flames towering toward the heavens. My lone picture is not that impressive.

Thankfully, no one was hurt since the explosion was in a field. The explosion was felt thirty or more miles away. It was about seven miles from where I live.

By three o'clock, the sky darkened again, and I headed back home. Soon, the night settled back into a peaceful November evening, and my heart rate returned to normal.

The view from my French doors today is still the calm wooded area it was yesterday. For that, I am most thankful.

Rock the Cradle—and Check for Alzheimer's

When we hold a newborn baby in our arms, we look into his or her eyes and wonder what kind of life is ahead for this new being. Our job as parents is to protect our children and keep them from harm. We shower them with love and envision how their future can reach greater heights than we ever did.

We worry about the little things—stomach aches that make the baby uncomfortable and cause him to cry. We may worry about childhood diseases and make appointments for immunizations.

Unless a family has a serious inherited genetic disease, most parents don't worry about what diseases their newborn might face later in life. Now, a new study may add to the list of new parental worries. Researchers have been looking for Alzheimer's in the most unlikely place—in the brains of infants.

The tests on sixty-two infants aged two to twenty-two months began with a DNA test to determine which ones had the gene variant APOE-E4, a risk factor for Alzheimer's disease. Sixty of the infants had the gene variant. MRI scans were used to measure activity in the infants' brains to compare the infants without the variation to the ones with it.

Oddly enough, differences were observed in the brain scans of the infants. The infants with the APOE-E4 variant had an increased brain growth in the frontal part of the brain with less growth in the middle and back parts of the brain. This is similar to the brain activity in adults who have Alzheimer's disease.

The type and number of copies a person has of the APOE (apolipoprotein E) allele is associated with the risk of developing late-onset Alzheimer's. The APOE gene has several functions, including carrying blood cholesterol through the body. APOE is found in neurons and brain cells in healthy brains and in plaques in the Alzheimer's brain. Three common alleles are E2, E3, and E4. E2 is thought to protect from Alzheimer's, E3 (the most common) is thought to be neutral, and E4 is linked to an increased risk of Alzheimer's. People with two E4 alleles, have a greater risk of developing Alzheimer's, but may not develop the disease, just as people without any of the E4 variant may develop the disease.

The good news is that although these infants have the APOE-E4 variant, it doesn't mean they will grow up to develop Alzheimer's late in life. Even better, the infants with the variant didn't show any developmental delays.

The study was intended to increase understanding of how the gene influences brain development. Sean Deoni, Brown University's Advanced Baby Imaging Lab, said, "These results do not establish a direct link to the changes seen in Alzheimer's patients, but with more research they may tell us something about how the gene contributes to Alzheimer's risk later in life."

The studies on infants are interesting and may be a piece of the puzzle when it comes to figuring out the genetic influence on Alzheimer's. Just like any disease influenced by genetics, environment may be the key to provide an override of the gene pool. Research shows that physical activity and good nutrition with healthy food choices can reduce the risk of Alzheimer's disease. Social interactions, puzzles, and brainteasers are ways to keep your brain active.

Our children complete the circle of life. We hope they inherit our good traits and healthy genes and the risk-carrying genes are allowed to sink into infinity.

When we rock the cradle, we need to worry less about genetic predispositions and concentrate on raising our children in a healthy environment.

A New Chapter

Some people embrace change while others participate after they're pulled into it kicking and screaming. I'm not sure that I fit totally into either category; I just know that the only thing that stays the same is that everything changes. Okay, so I may have borrowed that expression from a country song, but darn it, I'm sure I'd have thought of it eventually.

My life is about to change dramatically. After thirty-three years of driving to Central Missouri Electric each day to report to work, I'm embarking on that long-sought-after, scary, wildly dramatic change called "retirement." It's what I've worked and saved for throughout my career.

Most of my waking hours have been spent inside the doors of that building sitting in front of a computer monitor. Some days were more challenging that others, but my work career was one filled with learning new skills. I've done everything from data entry to management and had a rare opportunity to see the Coop move from a manual system into the world of computers.

Our computer programs were on an IBM System 34 and did not have such luxuries as word processing. Before we had PC's in the office, I typed the board minutes on a typewriter, and suffered through the frustration of having to retype an entire page if I left out a word. I'll admit, I hated to give up the Smart System for Word Perfect, then later to "downgrade" to Word. After seeing those gigantic columnar ledgers that Ann Richards and Grace Arbuckle used, it gave me a much greater respect for spreadsheets.

I saw a lot of changes during my years at the Coop, and in retrospect, I'll admit that most of them were for the better. Changes in my job kept it from ever becoming stale or boring. Even the people changed. I went from being the newbie, the first office employee to be hired in seven years, to being the person who had worked at the Coop the longest. That means I was working with a different set of people than those who were there when I first began.

There wasn't a lot of turnover and most of us worked together for several years. Co-workers became family—some are like brothers and sisters, others are like crazy aunts or uncles, or distant cousins. Just like family, you learn their quirks and learn to accept that as a part of the person, or better yet find humor in individual personalities.

At the employee/Christmas dinner, Kathy Page said I was getting ready to start a new chapter. For an avid reader and dedicated writer, that's the perfect description for how I feel about retirement—a new chapter in a good book—one that keeps me turning the pages. It's a book I don't want to put down, I find it intriguing, mysterious, suspenseful and I keep flipping pages wanting to know what's going to happen yet. My mind is rife with anticipation, excitement, and plans for what will happen next. My life's book is filled with rich characters who move in and out of the pages, imprinting their images on my heart, filling my days with love and laughter.

Just like a good book, my life has been a quest, and a journey, into the unknown to conquer all kinds of evil and overcome failures. Like all good stories, the protagonist in my story (me) is flawed, makes mistakes, passes up opportunities, often misses the mark, but still manages to overcome those itty bitty character flaws to be triumphant in a small way.

Is this going to be a new chapter, or an entirely new book? It seems that retirement is, in a way, a happy conclusion to one book, and time to begin a new one. Oh, sure it's going to be a series with many of the same characters, but a new set of adventures. Keep reading, because this new book promises to take a few strange twists and pack some surprises along the way.

'Tis the Season

'Tis the season to be _____. How would you fill in that blank? Of course, you may have the Fa, La, La, La song to convince you the word has to be "jolly." The problem with Christmas and *Jolly* are they don't always go together.

By its very nature, Christmas is a time of nostalgia, and folks, I'm here to tell you that nostalgia can be a dangerous, depressing emotion. If you have happy memories, you are sad because the past was happier than the present. If you have sad memories, you can become downhearted from thinking about it. It's easily a lose, lose situation.

It's also the season for stress on steroids. People are stressed about everything during the holidays second guessing themselves. *Did I spend too much? Did I spend too little? Did I buy the right size? Will he hate it? OMG, hope she put a gift receipt in here so I can take this back.*

And how many times have I pulled out the wrapping paper, scissors, bows, ribbons, and ho-ho-ho not a piece of tape in the house. *Maybe I could hold this sucker together with all those address labels that every charitable organization in the United States sends me.* A word from the wise—don't do it!

Don't forget all the Christmas events that may or may not be cancelled. The weather is always dicey this time of year. The Christmas parade was tossed forward from week to week until we ran out of weeks. I remember the years I worked on Christmas floats for Alzheimer's and then later for my women's group. It seems that I've always been fortunate enough to work in an unheated miserably cold building. I can't even imagine the frustration of going through all that work just to have the weather throw a hissy fit every week-end in December.

Nothing says holiday season like hazardous roadways. Throw in a little freezing rain and a half-foot of snow and it is a fool's errand to rush around trying to buy those last minute presents. Then, I can't help but ask myself—did I, or did I not, buy something at Target when I was in there a few weeks ago? I hardly ever shop at Target, but there I was…just at the perfect time for the credit/debit card bandits to strike.

It's really a lot easier to enjoy Christmas when you reduce the pressure. I've tried to get my shopping list pared down to the bare bones. Just buying for the sake of buying isn't my idea of fun. And those long lines snaking around the buildings while the wind chill is 40 below…no way! On Thanksgiving Day, no less. Black Friday was seriously anti-climatic after all the stores decided to skip being thankful for pushing the bargains. That darn Christmas stuff was out before Halloween. I wouldn't be surprised if the Labor Day sales next year are the beginning of the Christmas Shopping Season. Why not just move it up to Independence Day? Firecrackers and tinsel. They do kind of go together, don't you think?

Don't get me wrong. I'm not down on Christmas; it just doesn't always seem to be the magical time of year for me. Oh, I enjoy Christmas lights and Christmas carols just as much as the next person. I've become a Hallmark Christmas Movie addict. The thing I love most is having my family over for our annual Christmas get-together. It's a laid back, no pressure, big pot of chili good time. The reason I enjoy Christmas is because I have no expectations, I refuse to wax nostalgic, and I celebrate it without fanfare.

The one thing I don't care about is all that pressure to be, you guessed it, *jolly*. I'll be happy because I choose to hold that emotion in my heart whether it's Christmas or any of the other 364 days of the year. I'm a happy person. Jolly? Not so much.

A Blast from the Past

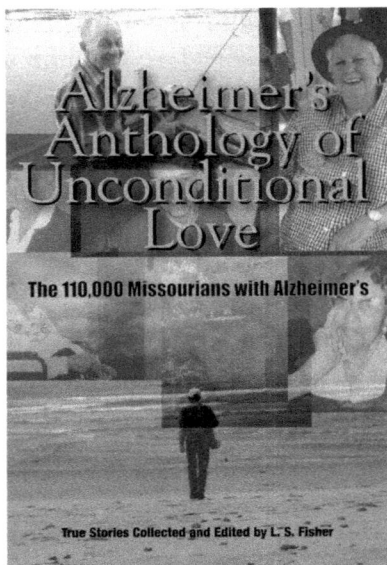

Alzheimer's Anthology of Unconditional Love

The 110,000 Missourians with Alzheimer's

True Stories Collected and Edited by L. S. Fisher

What better way to end the year than with a blast from the past?

I checked my PO Box yesterday and found an order for *Alzheimer's Anthology of Unconditional Love*. It was obviously from the ad that ran in *Rural Missouri* in 2007 when the book first came out. It happens occasionally. Someone is browsing through their old copies, come across the ad, and order a book.

This afternoon, I went into Facebook and saw where someone posted a note on a vote for my blog in Healthline's contest, "Did you see the ad for Linda's book in *Rural Missouri*?" What? I had just gotten my *Rural Missouri* today. I pulled it out, leafed through it, and there was the ad. Looks just as good as it did when the book was hot off the press.

The story of the anthology is a story in itself. I had never published a book before, but after joining the Columbia Chapter of the Missouri Writers' Guild, I learned a lot about self-publishing. I married that with my fundraising experience and came up with the idea to get sponsors, publish a book of Alzheimer's stories, and give the proceeds to the Alzheimer's Association. I pitched the idea to the staff at the Mid-Missouri

Chapter office and they didn't think I was crazy, so I proceeded.

One small problem to overcome. How could I get the stories? I sent emails to all my Alzheimer's contacts, posted on message boards, and spread the word. Then, Jim McCarty of *Rural Missouri* asked me to write an op-ed about Alzheimer's and the anthology. Once it was published, the stories came pouring in. The Chapter made the selections, and I began to build a book of compelling slice-of-life stories about our friends and neighbors who met Alzheimer's up close and personal. These were the stories of caregivers' unconditional love and the courage of those diagnosed with the disease.

Sandy Jaffe, the owner of BookSource and an Alzheimer's advocate I met at the Alzheimer's Forum in Washington, D.C., offered his expertise. He became my hero in this story. He hired a cover designer, found a distributor, and a printer. He called in favors and the book was published at no personal cost for me or the Alzheimer's Association. Proceeds would be pure profit. Before long, we sold the first 1,000 copies and began the process for the second printing.

Just when I thought the books were about all gone, Sandy found some in his warehouse and sent them to me. So, luckily, I have plenty of books to fill any orders the ad might generate.

By the way, if you don't get the *Rural Missouri* and would like to order a copy of *Alzheimer's Anthology of Unconditional Love: The 110,000 Missourians with Alzheimer's* the information is on my Website at www.lsfisher.com, or you can send $10 + $2.50 shipping to me at PO Box 1746, Sedalia MO 65302. Please make your checks payable to Alzheimer's Association.

Maybe the blast-from-the-past ad will bring in some funds for the Alzheimer's Association to help them further their mission. As we leave the past behind and move on to a New Year, let's each of us resolve to do our part to make this a better world for those who have dementia.

How can you join the fight against Alzheimer's? Lace up your shoes and participate in a Walk to End Alzheimer's next fall, visit a loved one with the disease, help a caregiver, write your senators and representatives about Alzheimer's research funding, or make a donation to your local Alzheimer's Chapter. If each of us takes one small step, we can circle the globe with love for those with the disease and create hope for a world without Alzheimer's.

Alzheimer's Anthology of Unconditional Love

Edited by L. S. Fisher

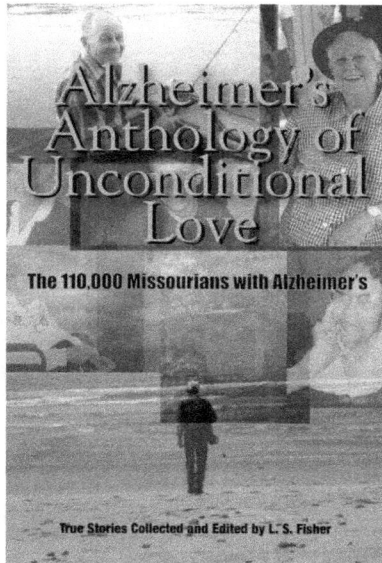

Mozark Press
PO Box 1746
Sedalia, MO 65302

www.lsfisher.com
www.MozarkPress.com

Early Onset Blog: Essays from an Online Journal

By L. S. Fisher

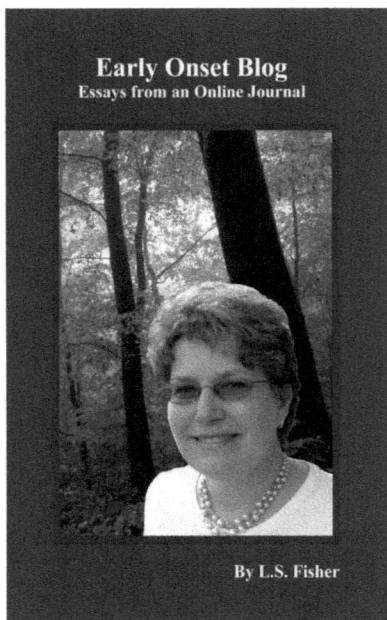

Mozark Press
PO Box 1746
Sedalia, MO 65302

www.lsfisher.com

Early Onset Blog: The Friendship Connection
&
Other Essays

By L. S. Fisher

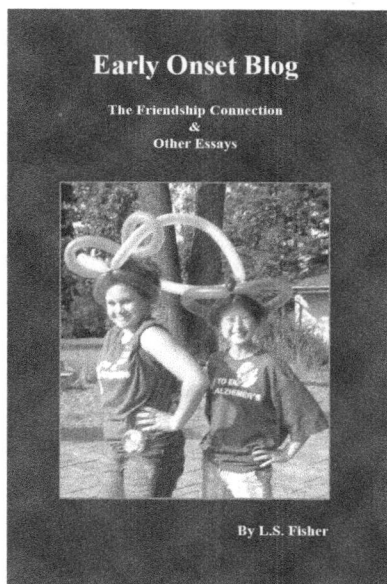

Mozark Press
PO Box 1746
Sedalia, MO 65302

www.MozarkPress.com
www.lsfisher.com

Early Onset Alzheimer's
Encourage, Inspire, and Inform

By L. S. Fisher

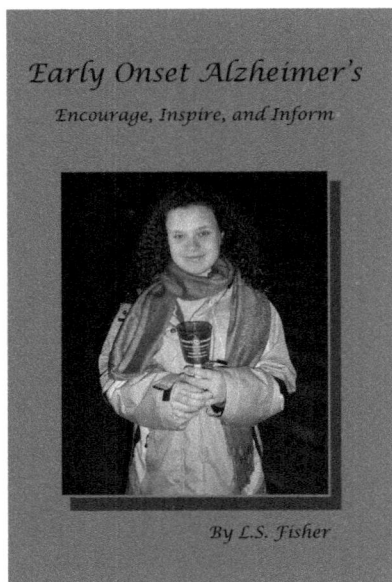

Mozark Press
PO Box 1746
Sedalia, MO 65302

www.MozarkPress.com
www.lsfisher.com

Early Onset Alzheimer's
My Recollections, Our Memories

By L. S. Fisher

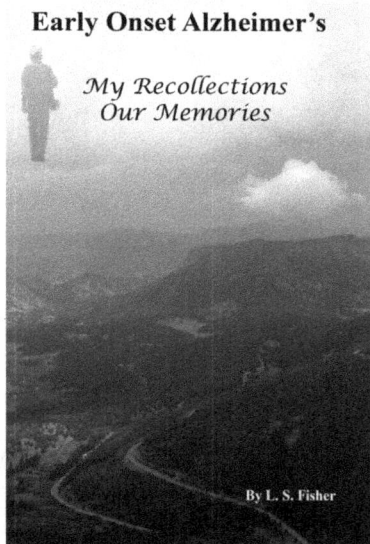

Mozark Press
PO Box 1746
Sedalia, MO 65302

www.MozarkPress.com
www.lsfisher.com

Focus on the Positive
Inspire, Encourage, and Inform

By L. S. Fisher

Mozark Press
PO Box 1746
Sedalia, MO 65302

www.MozarkPress.com
www.lsfisher.com

```
┌─────────────────────┐
│   Memory Talk       │      **Linda Fisher**
└──────┐──────────────┘      **Alzheimer's Speaker**
       \
        \
```

Author and Editor
of
Alzheimer's Anthology of Unconditional Love

Linda is a longtime Alzheimer's Association volunteer and advocate. She speaks from her personal experience as a primary caregiver for her husband who lived with early onset dementia for ten years. She will speak to your group or organization about Alzheimer's or writing life stories. Choose from the following presentations, or request a different Alzheimer's or writing topic:

Writing as Therapy: Rocks and Pebbles

Where are your real life stories? Learn how to reconnect with the pebbles of your life and how writing these stories can be therapeutic. Discover slice-of-life moments that only you know. Suitable for senior adult writing groups, caregivers, and support groups.

Alzheimer's Voices of Experience

Learn about Alzheimer's from short excerpts of the heartfelt stories collected in *Alzheimer's Anthology of Unconditional Love*. These true stories allow you to glimpse the lives of real people who have embarked upon an unwilling journey into the world of dementia. This presentation gives a face and voice to the statistics of a baffling disease. Suitable for nursing home staff, caregivers, Alzheimer's staff and volunteers, civic organizations, and people who want to know more about dementia.

Alzheimer's Can Happen at Any Age

A PowerPoint presentation that focuses on raising awareness that Alzheimer's is a neurological brain disease and not a normal part of aging. Suitable for nursing home staff, caregivers, Alzheimer's staff and volunteers, civic organizations, and people who want to know more about dementia.

Alzheimer's Caregivers: Survive and Thrive

A workshop to develop caregiver coping skills. Linda speaks from her personal experience as a primary caregiver for her husband who lived with early onset dementia for ten years. Suitable for caregivers.

Alzheimer's Caregiver Stress

A PowerPoint presentation covering signs of stress and stress management techniques. Linda learned coping skills from her personal experience as a primary caregiver for her husband. Suitable for caregivers and support groups.

Alzheimer's Communication: Hear their Voices

A presentation to develop communication skills. Linda draws on her experience as the primary caregiver for her husband and his difficulty communicating due to aphasia. Suitable for nursing home staff, caregivers, volunteers, and civic organizations.

To schedule a presentation:

Email: lfisher@lsfisher.com

From the Author

My therapist is on call twenty-four hours a day. Some of my most successful sessions occur in the middle of the night when I'm comfortable in my pajamas. I grab a pen and paper or fire up my laptop and write through my worries, hurt, or anger.

I began journaling when I was twelve years old, and

knew that writing helped me collect my thoughts and look at my problems more objectively. After I married and began to raise a family, I put away my journals except for an occasional travel log.

When my husband Jim developed dementia at forty-nine, I felt the need to write again. Through the ten years of Jim's dementia, I kept a detailed journal, mostly on tape. When I later transcribed the tapes, I re-discovered a wealth of information to help me heal.

Just like talking to a therapist, writing eased me through the emotionally draining decade of Jim's illness. The power of the pen healed my spirit.

Gathering and editing stories for *Alzheimer's Anthology of Unconditional Love* gave me purpose after Jim's death. I'm still working on a memoir and hope these stories can help others along their journeys.

My love of writing complements my volunteer work and helps me focus on the power of positive thinking and action.

L. S. Fisher lives, works, and writes in Sedalia, MO. The greatest tragedy in her life led to her greatest accomplishments. If her husband had not developed dementia, she would have spent her days working and her evenings at home. Instead, she has been recognized locally, statewide, and nationally for her Alzheimer's Association volunteer work.

Website: www.lsfisher.com
Blog: http://earlyonset.blogspot.com

Essay originally published in *Bylines 2010 Writer's Desk Calendar*, Snowflake Press, www.bylinescalendar.com

MoZark Press
Sedalia, Missouri

Mozark Press is a small publishing company in central Missouri dedicated to producing quality paperback books. We will publish short story collections, inspirational works, anthologies, general fiction, and non-fiction.

Mozark Press plans to publish 1-5 new books per year that meet our standards. We expect manuscripts to be polished and error-free when submitted.

Contact us if you want to see your work in print, but haven't been successful with a major publishing company. Maybe you have considered self-publishing, but do not have the time or know-how to do it yourself. We've been there, done that, and wouldn't wish it on anyone.

We are interested in new or established authors. Mozark Press will partner with our authors. We will provide a complimentary author webpage for one year. We won't ask you to sign a long-term contract.

We do not accept unsolicited manuscripts. If you have a completed manuscript, you would like us to consider, send a query letter to:

Publisher@mozarkpress.com

www.ingramcontent.com/pod-product-compliance
Lightning Source LLC
Chambersburg PA
CBHW071534040426
42452CB00008B/1010